GARDENING
SHORTCUTS

LONDON, NEW YORK, MUNICH, MELBOURNE, DELHI

PROJECT EDITOR Lee Wilson
PROJECT ART EDITOR Alison Gardner
PICTURE RESEARCH Rose Horridge, Susie Peachey,
Romaine Werblow
PRODUCTION EDITORS Sarah Isle, Clare McLean
PRODUCTION CONTROLLER Claire Pearson
JACKET DESIGN Nicola Powling
MANAGING EDITOR Penny Warren
MANAGING ART EDITOR Alison Donovan
PUBLISHER Mary Ling
ART DIRECTOR Peter Luff

PHOTOGRAPHY Peter Anderson, Brian North

US EDITOR Rebecca Warren

First American Edition, 2012

Published in the United States by
DK Publishing, 375 Hudson Street,
New York, New York 10014

12 13 14   10 9 8 7 6 5 4 3 2 1

001—181301—Mar/2012

Published in Great Britain by Dorling Kindersley Limited.

A catalog record for this book is available from the
Library of Congress.

ISBN 978 0 7566 8978 0

DK books are available at special discounts when purchased
in bulk for sales promotions, premiums, fund-raising, or
educational use. For details, contact: DK Publishing Special
Markets, 375 Hudson Street, New York, New York, 10014 or
SpecialSales@dk.com.

Printed and bound by Leo Paper Products Ltd, China

Important notice
The authors and publishers can accept no liability for any harm,
damage, or illness arising from the use or misuse of the plants
described in this book.

Discover more at
www.dk.com

GARDENING
SHORTCUTS

Jenny Hendy

Contents

Introduction

Relaxed patios

Beautiful borders

Smart features

Grow it, eat it

Better boundaries

Welcoming wildlife

Easy care

Introduction

With all that we cram into our lives, it is hardly surprising that gardening often takes a back seat, but working in the fresh air, growing your own food, and exploring personal creativity are great ways to combat stress.

Life in the fast lane

Most of us would prefer to have more time to relax and enjoy being outdoors rather than feeling like a slave to the garden. Fortunately, this book can not only help you improve your plot, but perhaps even give you some time to spare.

It all adds up

Broken down into bite-sized activities, *Gardening Shortcuts* is easy to follow even if you don't have previous experience. Projects and tasks are organized to achieve a whole lot of gardening in short time frames.

The timer symbol indicates activities that can be completed in 30 minutes or less once the the preliminaries like soil preparation and watering have been taken care of. If you can fit several 30-minute sessions into a week, you will soon start to see real progress.

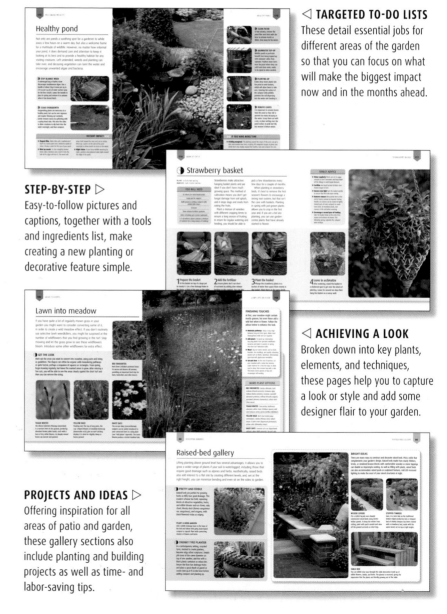

◁ TARGETED TO-DO LISTS
These detail essential jobs for different areas of the garden so that you can focus on what will make the biggest impact now and in the months ahead.

STEP-BY-STEP ▷
Easy-to-follow pictures and captions, together with a tools and ingredients list, make creating a new planting or decorative feature simple.

◁ ACHIEVING A LOOK
Broken down into key plants, elements, and techniques, these pages help you to capture a look or style and add some designer flair to your garden.

PROJECTS AND IDEAS ▷
Offering inspiration for all areas of patio and garden, these gallery sections also include planting and building projects as well as time- and labor-saving tips.

BASIC TOOLS

If you gather together a basic kit of garden tools and supplies and keep them in one place, you won't waste time looking for tools, borrowing them, or making do with implements not suited to the task. Treat yourself to a good-quality stainless-steel hand trowel and fork, and buy a pair of shears that suit your hand size and grip. Having a range of supplies in stock also means you won't have to go shopping every time you want to garden. A garden shed, locker, or built-in storage space is ideal for keeping everything together.

HANDY SUPPLIES

* ❋ **Gel crystals** These water-retaining crystals turn into a gel when water is added, helping to keep compost moist.

* ❋ **Granular fertilizer** Use a general-purpose fertilizer to improve soil before planting new areas or when dividing perennials. Slow-release fertilizers will last longer.

* ❋ **Liquid fertilizer** Dilute concentrated feeds and apply with a watering can, or buy ready mixed.

* ❋ **Glyphosate weedkiller** A ready-to-use hand sprayer is very useful for spot-treating tricky perennial weeds.

* ❋ **Garden twine** Tie in climber stems and support tall herbaceous perennials with twine and stakes.

* ❋ **Multi-purpose compost** Keep a bag with added soil-based compost for container plantings.

* ❋ **Crocks and gravel** These provide drainage in pots and planters (see over). Crocks can be broken pieces of clay pots, stones, or you can even use broken-up styrofoam packaging.

* ❋ **Ornamental bark** Mulching with bark helps retain moisture and suppress weeds. Top off any thin patches regularly.

* ❋ **Oil can and rags** Keep a can of lubricating, anti-corrosion product and a rag for lubricating, waterproofing, and rust-proofing cutting tools.

1. spade for digging planting holes and distributing manure and mulches; **2. fork** for weeding, aerating lawns, and breaking up compacted soil; **3. brush** for sweeping soil and debris from hard surfaces and dispersing worm casts; **4. garden rake** for preparing and leveling soil for sowing, etc.; **5. spring tine rake** for scarifying turf and clearing up fall leaves; **6. half-moon cutter** for cutting and re-edging lawns; **7. shears** for clipping hedges and topiary, as well as neatening herbs and perennials; **8. clippers** for deadheading and pruning; **9. pruning saw** a small foldaway model for medium stems; a large pruning saw or bow saw for bigger branches; **10. old knife** for easing out tap-rooted weeds in lawns; also for paving joints; **11. scissors** for cutting twine, deadheading, and harvesting vegetables and fresh flowers; **12. plastic trug** (flexible container with handles) for plunging plants prior to planting, moving compost, and collecting weeds and clippings; **13. watering can** for watering in new plantings and applying diluted fertilizers; **14. lawnmower** choose an appropriate size for your garden; **15. string trimmer** for neatening long grass by boundaries and cutting meadows after flowering

Nitty gritty

Basic ground and container preparation, planting, sowing, and watering instructions are given here to avoid repeating the same advice in each step-by-step sequence. The timing of the projects assumes that you have completed these preparations; gathered all the necessary tools, supplies, and plant material; and are ready to go! Common tools are not included in the "You will need" list.

SPOTTING YOUR SOIL TYPE

Knowing your soil type and its pH (acidity or alkalinity) allows you to choose suitable plants. Buy a pH test kit to see if you have acidic (suitable for lime-hating, ericaceous plants), neutral, or alkaline soil. If your sample feels gritty and crumbles under pressure, it is sandy and typically free-draining. Heavy clay can be rolled and formed into a ring. It normally drains poorly.

SANDY SOIL

CLAY SOIL

pH LEVEL

GROUND PREPARATION

If soil is compacted, break it up by digging or forking over and reducing large clods. Don't dig clay if it is too dry since this destroys the crumblike structure, making it even more poorly drained and likely to dry like concrete.

REMOVE WEEDS
Clear annuals by hand. Dig out or spray perennials with weedkillers.

ORGANIC MATTER
Fork well-rotted manure or garden compost into the area to be planted.

FERTILIZER
Add slow-release fertilizer to the soil according to the packet instructions and mix in well.

FIRMING IN
Press loose soil down around the root ball using the flat of your hands.

WATERING
Soak the area around new plantings to settle soil around the roots.

CONTAINER PLANTING

Larger pots and baskets need less watering than smaller ones and also have room for roots to grow, which in turn supports top growth. Leave a gap between the compost surface and the top of the pot to allow water to pool; this gives the water time to soak in.

DRAINAGE HOLES
It is essential for pots and baskets to have drainage holes. Drill or punch holes through.

LINING POTS
Add an insulating liner to metal pots to protect roots from temperature extremes.

PRE-PLANTING SOAK
Push root balls below the surface of the water, and wait until the bubble stream stops.

CROCKS
Use broken clay-pot pieces, stone shards, or large gravel to cover holes.

PLANTING DEPTH
Use a pole to check that the root ball surface is level with the surrounding soil.

MULCHING
Apply 3in (8cm) of bark chips to prevent weeds and aid in moisture retention.

SOWING SEEDS

Whether sowing direct in the ground or in trays and pots, sow as thinly as possible to give plants space to grow properly. For indoor sowing, use sterilized seed compost.

SEED DRILL
Rake the surface to fine crumbs. Make a shallow line (drill), sow, and then lightly cover.

THINNING
Keep your seeds watered. Once seedlings emerge, thin some out to give others more room.

PRICKING OUT
If sowing in trays indoors, transplant seedlings to individual pots to keep growing.

BUYING PLANTS

❊ **Label check** Read plant labels to find eventual height and spread; soil and sun preferences; whether the plant is hardy for your area; and if it is perennial (lives from year to year) or annual (completes its life cycle in one year and dies).

❊ **Picking good specimens** Select well-balanced plants with good foliage cover that have been kept well watered. Check for any sign of pests or disease. Avoid root-bound plants (roots matted beneath pot) or ones with exposed roots on the surface or that have lots of weeds.

❊ **Perfect plants** Buy flowering plants in bud or that are just starting to bloom. Select plants that show signs of new growth. Gently remove from the pot to check for a healthy root system.

❊ **Plants to avoid** Never buy half-hardy bedding plants or tender perennials if they are being sold outdoors without protection when spring weather is still frosty. Avoid any with dead or diseased stems or distorted or discolored leaves (a sign of insect, virus problems, nutrient disorder, or frost injury).

Relaxed patios

During the warmer months the patio or terrace becomes an extension of the house or apartment— a place to sit and enjoy the fresh air, to cook and eat meals with friends and family, and to entertain. It's well worth focusing some attention on making this an intimate and beautiful day- and nighttime space with pots and planters to provide color, sculptural form, and fragrance.

Spruce up your patio

In most properties the deck or patio is the link between the house and garden. Any paved area or deck can have a lovely roomlike feel, provided you pay a little attention to detail. De-cluttering, tidying, and cleaning are just as important here as indoors. The key to a speedy patio makeover is to cast a critical eye over the whole space and target the most urgent jobs. Dead plants, fading flowers, and limp leaves draw the eye for all the wrong reasons, so deal with these eyesores promptly, and prune unruly growth.

KEEP IN SHAPE

Lightly trim potted topiary, removing clippings from the plant and soil to reduce disease problems. Remove multiple spent blooms, and shape alpines, shrubby herbs, and tender perennials using hand shears. Cut off over-long trailing shoots to keep arrangements in balance.

FADED GLORY

Remove unattractive brown blooms and yellow leaves. Use pruners or flower scissors to deadhead larger faded flowers, and pull out or trim the dead centers of flower clusters on plants like pot geraniums. Remove the flower stalks of long-stemmed faded blooms.

INSTANT IMPACT <<

❋ **Quick color** Bring out cushions and throws to add a sense of luxury as well as color.

❋ **Top dressing** Dress the tops of your pots with slate chips, pebbles, or gravel to create a fresh new look. Scatter the same material artfully around the base of a group of pots.

❋ **Clean furniture** Spot-clean marks and stuck-on debris on tables and chairs with some warm soapy water and a soft-bristled brush.

❋ **Toss it** Scoop up litter or debris, and take organic matter to the compost bin. Use a small hand brush for reaching awkward corners.

🕐 CLIMBER CONTROL

Tie new shoots of climbers and wall shrubs onto their wire or trellis supports. Prune off any less flexible stems that are growing outward or that hang too low beneath pergola crossbeams and arches.

🕐 CLEAN SWEEP

Do a whirlwind sweep of all paved and decked surfaces. A soft-bristled indoor broom handles easier than a stiff yard broom. Remove debris from gravel or slate chips with a plastic rake or leaf blower.

🕐 POT REVIVAL

Move planters around to maximize displays (groups of three work well), and replace individual dead or fading plants with fresh ones. Give pots a good soak using a hose with a lance attachment for ease. Follow up with ready-mixed liquid fertilizer.

🕐 WEED THEM OUT

Hand pull or use an old knife to scrape out any weeds that are growing in cracks between paving stones or through gravel surfaces. Alternatively, spot treat with a ready-mixed glyphosate weedkiller spray.

>> IF YOU HAVE MORE TIME

❋ **Plant swap** Completely replant any tired-looking patio containers with new plant arrangements placed in removable plastic pot "liners." This will make it easier in the future to swap faded planters with inserts nurtured in the wings.

❋ **Scrub the decks** Scrub away algae and moss from your paving or decking using a commercial cleaning fluid.

Spring planting

YOU WILL NEED

Drainage material (see pp.8–9)

Multi-purpose potting compost with added soil-based compost

Colored ceramic container

3 x dwarf daffodils (*Narcissi*)

3 x pots gold-lace primulas

1 x black mondo grass (*Ophiopogon planiscapus* 'Nigrescens')

By matching a colorful container with a coordinated group of spring plants, the impact created by a single patio pot is so much greater. Here the yellow of the daffodils picks up on the color of the beautifully marked gold lace primulas, whose dark markings are echoed by the almost black grassy leaves of *Ophiopogon planiscapus* 'Nigrescens'. Think about the likely backdrop to a planter when you are putting a design together. In this case the blue stained fence in the background makes an ideal foil for both the yellow pot and the yellow flowers.

Spring bedding planted in the fall can suffer over the winter, and by planting a few pots with instant-impact bulbs and bedding once the weather warms up in the spring, the arrangements will look nice and fresh. These plants tolerate sun or light shade.

1 Prepare the pot
Cover the pot holes with small rocks, then add some compost so that the largest plants are setting at the right height. Leave a gap between the top of the root ball and the rim to allow for watering.

2 Position the centerpiece
After thoroughly soaking the plants, take the daffodils out of their pots, and set at the back of the planter. Place primulas on either side of the daffodils and one in front. Ensure they are upright.

3 Add the other plants
Take the black mondo grass out of its pot, and split the wiry root system with your hands, breaking off clumps of leaves and roots to squeeze in between the primulas. Work compost into the gaps.

MORE PLANT OPTIONS

❊ **Bulb centerpiece** Choose medium height daffodils, like the orange-centered 'Jetfire', or hyacinths. The tulip 'Red Riding Hood' has showy, weather-resistant blooms and marbled leaves, and other early tulips like 'Purissima' (white) or 'Toronto' (pink) will also last well.

❊ **Middle tier** Surround the bulbs with single-color bedding primulas; double daisy (*Bellis perennis*); grape hyacinth (*Muscari armeniacum*); pansies; or *Chionodoxa* 'Pink Giant'.

❊ **Foliage contrast** Try English ivies (*Hedera helix*); for bronze purple leaves try *Ajuga reptans* 'Braunherz' or 'Catlin's Giant' or the sedge *Carex flagellifera*; for bold striped leaves, try yellow-striped *Carex oshimensis* 'Evergold'.

4 Water well

Check all around the plants, lifting the leaves of the primulas to see if you've left any spaces between the root balls. Water plants gently to settle the compost, and fill any gaps as necessary.

Spring pots

It might take a while for borders to start showing color after winter, but your patio pots can be like a spring prelude. In the sheltered environment of a sunny patio or deck, sumptuous potted tulips and other spring blooms can perform far better than they might if they were in a more exposed or poorly drained spot in the main garden.

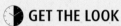 **GET THE LOOK**

This elegant design departs from the normal spring palette of blue, white, and yellow. Plant the large perennial wallflower *Erysimum* 'Bowles's Mauve' at the back of a well-draining terra-cotta pot containing loam-based potting compost. Add three *Euphorbia amygdaloides* 'Purpurea' for foliage contrast in the foreground. Plant another, slightly shorter clay pot with three Tulip 'Zurel' or similar, in bud, and squeeze in 5–6 *Senecio cineraria* 'Silver Dust'.

FOLIAGE SPARKLE
The silver, finely cut foliage of the hardy evergreen *Senecio cineraria* 'Silver Dust' lifts darker tones and works particularly well with whites and pastels.

FLAMBOYANT TOUCH
The tulip 'Zurel' with its two-tone feather-patterned petals is particularly eye-catching. Garden centers offer a range of tulips ready to bloom for instant effect.

BACKGROUND BLOOM
The hardy, shrublike wallflower *Erysimum* 'Bowles's Mauve' flowers from spring through to summer, and the profusion of small blooms creates the perfect backdrop for bold tulips.

DARK MATTER
The dusky leaves of *Euphorbia amygdaloides* 'Purpurea' echo the deep purple markings of the tulip. Lime greenflower heads add "zing."

FINISHING TOUCHES

Settle the plants in by watering. Consider placing the tulip pots straight into the larger pot so you can change them when they fade.

❋ **Before and after** Plant early *Crocus chrysanthus* around the pot rim, and pick a later tulip like 'Ballade' to extend the look.

❋ **Shrubby shelter** Provide a protected area for delicate blooms using tough potted evergreen shrubs and conifers.

MORE PLANT OPTIONS

FOLIAGE SPARKLE *Artemisia stelleriana* 'Boughton Silver'; *Brunnera macrophylla* 'Jack Frost'; *Convolvulus cneorum*; English ivy (*Hedera helix*) white-marbled cultivars; *Heuchera* 'Silver Scrolls'; *Lamium maculatum* 'White Nancy'; *Pulmonaria saccharata* Argentea Group

FLAMBOYANT TOUCH Crown imperial (*Fritillaria imperialis* cultivars); double daffodils e.g. *Narcissus* 'Sir Winston Churchill', 'Tahiti'; parrot tulips; Tulip 'Aladdin' (lily-flowered); Tulip 'Angélique' (double, late)

BACKGROUND BLOOM Bleeding heart (*Dicentra spectabilis*) and *Dicentra* 'Stuart Boothman'; dwarf rhododendron; perennial wallflower (*Erysimum* 'Constant Cheer'); *Viola* Sorbet Series; winter heathers (*Erica carnea* and *Erica* x *darleyensis* cultivars)

DARK MATTER *Ajuga reptans* 'Braunherz' or 'Catlin's Giant'; *Euphorbia dulcis* 'Chameleon'; *Viola riviniana* Purpurea Group; *Heuchera* 'Licorice' and 'Obsidian'; bronze fennel (*Foeniculum vulgare* 'Purpureum'—new shoots); black mondo grass (*Ophiopogon planiscapus* 'Nigrescens')

Summer pots

By grouping containers of annual bedding and tender perennial patio plants together like this, you can create a mini garden. The effect is more successful when you keep to a simple color scheme. This elegant look uses yellows, white, blue, and silver, but if you prefer a hot mix, why not try orange, deep red, and hot pink mingled with purple, bronze, and lime?

◕ GET THE LOOK

Plant one Marguerite daisy (*Argyranthemum frutescens*) into a 12in (30cm) terra-cotta pot filled with multi-purpose compost mixed with soil-based compost. Using a 10in (25cm) pot, plant three pale yellow Surfinia petunias and one *Helichrysum petiolare* 'Limelight' together. In a similar pot, plant one *Osteospermum* 'Whirlygig'. Plant the three *Isotoma axillaris* in a 9in (23cm) pot. Position them in a group with the smaller pots in front.

FLOWER POWER
Petunias offer non-stop flowers all summer provided they are regularly deadheaded and treated to a generous regime of watering and feeding with liquid plant food.

FILLER PLANTS
Weaving colorful, small-flowered plants between bigger, showier specimens is a perfect way to tie the collection together. *Isotoma axillaris* is very effective.

FLOWERING SHRUB
Tender subshrubs like this yellow-flowered Marguerite daisy are able to stand above lower-growing patio plants, which helps create a more dynamic arrangement.

FINISHING TOUCHES

After planting, water pots and arrange them in a sunny spot. If you didn't use slow-release fertilizer, start feeding with liquid fertilizer six weeks after planting.

* **Tiered display** As the plants start to grow and become bushy, stand the larger pots on bricks, and set smaller ones at their base for a more eye-catching arrangement.
* **Dark backdrop** These pale-colored blooms stand out best against a contrasting backdrop, such as a painted fence or trimmed evergreens.
* **Plain floor** Fine gravel on the ground makes an ideal foil for the weathered pots and varied flowers and foliage. Plain paving or dark slate chips would also work well.
* **Intermingle** Add to the collection with another pot containing a silver *Helichrysum petiolare* and plain white or cream osteospermums. Let all the plants intermingle for an English-garden look.

FOLIAGE IMPACT
Don't just rely on flowering bedding plants to bring color to summer pots; foliage can also add interest, particularly using plants like *Helichrysum petiolare* 'Limelight'.

EYECATCHER
Some plants clamor for your attention, and *Osteospermum* 'Whirlygig' is one such example. Including an unusual flower or leaf shape like this helps your collection pop.

MORE PLANT OPTIONS

FLOWER POWER *Begonia* Illumination Series; *Bidens ferulifolia*; *Petunia* Tumbelina and Surfinia Series; trailing geranium (*Pelargonium* Mini Cascade Series); trailing *Verbena* Temari Series

FILLER PLANTS *Bacopa*; *Diascia*; *Lobelia*; *Nemesia*

FLOWERING SHRUBS French lavender (*Lavandula pedunculata* subsp. *pedunculata*); *Fuchsia*

FOLIAGE IMPACT *Solenostemon*; golden creeping Jenny (*Lysimachia nummularia* 'Aurea'); *Helichrysum petiolare* 'Variegatum'; *Lysimachia congestiflora* 'Outback Sunset'; *Perilla frutescens* var. *purpurascens*

EYECATCHER *Begonia* Bonfire; *Begonia* Million Kisses Series; *Fuchsia* 'Thalia'

Potted shrubs

Shrubs growing in containers add a feeling of maturity to a deck, courtyard, or patio. Larger specimens provide height and structure and can also help create privacy by acting as a living screen.

Evergreen shrubs offer interest in the winter when herbaceous perennials, tender bedding, and patio plants have faded. Some varieties will also provide long-lasting summer interest in the form of vibrant leaves or abundant blooms. All can be used either as a focal point or as part of a backdrop for pots of seasonal bulbs and flowers.

If you don't have the right soil conditions to grow acid-loving plants such as camellias, pieris, or rhododendrons, growing them in pots of acid-based compost with added soil-based compost is the perfect solution.

MORE PLANT OPTIONS

❈ **Eye-catching feature** Clip Boxwood (*Buxus sempervirens*) into a ball for an eye-catching feature on a shady terrace.

❈ **Mediterranean feel** French lavender (*Lavandula pedunculata* subsp. *pedunculata*) is a long-flowering, aromatic shrub for full sun, with violet blooms through summer.

❈ **Long-flowering display** *Hydrangea petiolaris* 'Preziosa' is a narrow-leaf mophead hydrangea, with dark stems and red-tinted foliage. It flowers in summer and fall; pink darkening to burgundy.

❈ **Stylishly delicate** Japanese maple (*Acer palmatum*) has delicately cut leaves in colors from deep purple to pale yellow, green, or amber. Shelter from wind.

❈ **Fragrant evergreen** Mexican orange (*Choisya* x *dewitteana* 'Aztec Pearl') is a compact evergreen with scented white flowers in early summer, often repeating.

1 Provide drainage
Cover the holes in the base of the pot with a few broken pot pieces or small rocks. This prevents compost from leaking through the holes or blocking them, which can stop drainage and cause waterlogging.

2 Add some compost
Pour in sufficient compost to allow the shrub to sit at the right height in the pot. Leave at least 1in (2½cm) between the top of the compost and the rim for watering, more if you are adding a gravel mulch.

3 Examine the roots
Plunge-water the plant (see pp.8–9), remove from the pot, and check the roots. Do not disturb the fine roots of well-grown shrubs, but gently loosen any thick roots wound around the base.

4 Center the shrub
Mix some slow-release fertilizer into the compost, and set the shrub in the middle of the pot. Backfill with compost to the level of its original pot. Firm lightly.

5 Water the planted pot
Gently water the pot to settle the compost around the roots. To avoid displacing the soil, pour the water over a piece of broken pot set on the surface.

6 Mulch with gravel
Scatter a layer of gravel on top of the compost to help keep down weeds. Fine chipped bark is a good choice for acid-loving, woodland species.

Fall pots

At this time of year garden centers offer a wide range of container plants, including annual types that need sheltering from colder nights as well as hardy shrubs and perennials for winter interest.

🕐 GET THE LOOK

Add drainage material to clay pots. The violas and ornamental kale require multi-purpose potting compost; the others are acid-loving plants and need acid-based compost. Plant and water well.

BEDDING SHADES

In this arrangement blue-flowered varieties of weather-resistant *Viola* Penny or Sorbet Series enhance the surrounding reds and purples. In a sheltered spot, with regular deadheading, it will bloom until spring.

TENDER TREATS

Although not a completely hardy plant, the papery flowers of Cape heather (*Erica gracilis*) will add a splash of vivid crimson or white to your design well into the winter.

EVERGREEN GLOSS

The combination of dark, glossy, sculpted foliage and crimson flower buds make the shrub *Skimmia japonica* 'Rubella' an ideal backdrop for more delicate blooms, such as mini cyclamen.

BERRY BLISS

Scarlet or blood-red berries, such as those of the creeping *Gaultheria procumbens* (the berries are poisonous), shine against a backdrop of deep green foliage. Plant these singly, or use as a filler.

LEAFY LUXURY

Deep-colored varieties of ornamental kale work well with rich fall tones. The bold, circular plant adds texture to the plan. Remove yellow leaves at the base of the rosettes.

FINISHING TOUCHES

The flowers and foliage of these plants are dramatic in their own right, but a little planning and careful positioning shows them at their best.

❊ **Rich mix** This display takes its inspiration from the rich hues of fall. The seasonal "glow" is achieved by combining crimson, purple, deep scarlet, and lustrous green.

❊ **Stepped display** Steps enable you to stage your display creatively. Place pots so foliage and flowers mask the sides of those behind. Alternatively, stand some pots on bricks or upturned containers to stagger their height.

❊ **Weathered pots** Terra-cotta weathers to a mellow finish that perfectly highlights this design's jewel colors. To hasten the process with new pots, stand in a damp, shady corner.

❊ **Sheltered corner** The warmth generated by house walls, especially beneath an open porch, often keeps pots frost-free, and helps extend the season of fall-bloomers.

MORE PLANT OPTIONS

BEDDING SHADES Fall-flowering pinks (*Dianthus*); snapdragon (*Antirrhinum majus*); dwarf double Michaelmas daisy (*Aster*)

TENDER TREATS Bedding dahlias; mini cyclamens; mini chrysanthemums; ornamental peppers

EVERGREEN GLOSS Bergenia 'Eric Smith'; ivy (*Hedera helix*); *Skimmia x confusa* 'Kew Green'

BERRY BLISS Cotoneaster salicifolius 'Gnom'; *Gaultheria mucronata*; *Skimmia japonica*

LEAFY LUXURY *Ajuga reptans* 'Burgundy Glow'; *Calluna vulgaris* 'Wickwar Flame'; *Choisya ternata* 'Sundance'; *Euonymus fortunei*; evergreen ferns; *Heuchera*; lesser periwinkle (*Vinca minor*); *Leucothoe* 'Scarletta'; *Leucothoe axillaris* 'Curly Red'; *Senecio cineraria* 'Silver Dust'

Winter pots

In the dark days of winter any bloom is treasured. Pots deserve a spot close to the house so they can be admired from within. This design sets pure white snowdrops against an array of dark, rich colors.

 GET THE LOOK

Fill a plastic pot with loam-based compost (pp.8–9). Place two pots of snowdrops at the back with a *Cyclamen coum* on either side and two *Iris reticulata* in the middle. In the front, put one *Primula* 'Wanda', and tuck three stems of ivy among the plants.

DARK DELIGHTS

These *Iris reticulata* appear at the same time as snowdrops, and the purple-blue, spidery blooms make an interesting contrast. Instead of planting them, put the bulbs, pot and all, into the soil, and remove after flowering.

FOLIAGE FOIL

In this dusky, wintry design there is a variety of interesting foliage colors. The glossy green of the ivy blends well with the marbled cyclamen and the leaves of the primula.

HARDY GEMS

This little cyclamen produces its mauve pink blooms in succession over marbled, heart-shaped foliage. Avoiding watering directly onto the plant's crown; this helps prevent rot.

WINTER BEDDING

Few bedding flowers thrive in cold weather, but in mild spells the relatively hardy Wanda Group primroses produce rich-colored blooms over dark green or bronze-tinged leaves.

PALE HARBINGER

There's nothing like snowdrops for letting us know that spring is near. Planting ready-grown potted bulbs guarantees a flowering display.

FINISHING TOUCHES

Water plants well, but avoid wetting the foliage, since this can encourage fungal problems. Stand the container in a sheltered, fairly sunny spot.

❊ **Basket** Place the plastic pot in a wicker basket, arranging the foliage over the rim.

❊ **Driftwood** Complete the picture by placing a piece of driftwood or a dark, moss-covered stone behind the basket as a backdrop.

MORE PLANT OPTIONS

DARK DELIGHTS *Crocus* 'Ladykiller'; *Crocus tommasinianus* 'Barr's Purple'; *Iris reticulata* varieties, e.g 'George', 'Harmony', 'Pixie', 'Purple Gem', 'Violet Beauty'; Siberian squill (*Scilla siberica* 'Spring Beauty')

FOLIAGE FOIL Black mondo grass (*Ophiopogon planiscapus* 'Nigrescens'); English ivy (*Hedera helix*), especially cut-leaf varieties such as 'Très Coupé' and 'Königer's Auslese'; *Uncinia uncinata rubra*

HARDY GEMS Hellebore hybrids (*Helleborus x hybridus*); primrose (*Primula vulgaris* and *Primula* Wanda Group); *Viola riviniana*

WINTER BEDDING Mini cyclamen (not frost hardy); *Primula* Wanda Group; *Viola* Sorbet Series

PALE HARBINGER *Crocus chrysanthus* 'Cream Beauty', *Crocus* 'Snow Bunting'; double snowdrop (*Galanthus nivalis* f. *pleniflorus*) 'Flore Pleno', and other snowdrop cultivars, e.g. 'Atkinsii' and 'Magnet'; *Iris reticulata*, e.g. pale blue-and-yellow streaked 'Katharine Hodgkin', white 'Natascha'.

Low-water pots

If you don't have time to water pots on a regular basis or are away from home for long periods, there are plants that will survive on a pretty meager supply. Succulents and alpines are experts at storing water in their leaves and stems or have other adaptations to reduce moisture loss.

◗ PLANTING A SUCCULENT-FILLED TEAPOT

Unlike most conventional pot plants that need a relatively large soil volume to keep their roots moist, succulents can survive in all kinds of small containers, even an old teapot. Try house leeks (*Sempervivum*), or hen and chicks (*Jovibarba*), some creeping sedums, and other rosette-forming succulents like the tender *Echeveria* species.

PLANTING POTS
Blend loam-based compost with 50 percent grit and horticultural sand. Ideally, drill a drainage hole in the teapot, but otherwise fill the pot with one-third drainage material and two-thirds compost mix, leaving space for planting. Add the succulent.

FINISHING OFF
Fill gaps around the root ball with more compost. Water sparingly. Cover bare soil surface with colored glass or acrylic chips, shells, or pebbles. Arrange a quirky grouping.

HANGING BALL
Fix two compost-filled hanging baskets together with wire, and plant small succulent offsets through from the outside.

BRIGHT IDEAS

With countless different *Sempervivum* to choose from, you can create attractive patio pots using just these plants. Why not plant adjacent paving cracks to match?

DISPLAYS

To show off your collections of alpines and succulents, consider investing in a tiered stand like this, or arrange pots and shallow alpine pans down a flight of steps.

MORE PLANT OPTIONS

❉ **Mediterranean feel** Try *Aeonium*; curry plant (*Helichrysum italicum*); *Echeveria*; house leek (*Sempervivum*); *Jovibarba*; rosemary (*Rosmarinus*); Spanish lavender (*Lavandula stoechas*)

❉ **Desertscape** Try these for a great desert feel: *Aloe*; *Haworthia*; Jade tree (*Crassula ovata*); prickly pear cactus (*Opuntia*); *Agave americana* 'Mediopicta'; *Yucca*

❉ **Alpine troughs** Atlas mountain daisy (*Anacyclus depressus*); creeping thyme (*Thymus*); *Delosperma nubigenum*; *Sedum* (creeping forms e.g. *Sedum spathulifolium* 'Purpureum' and 'Cape Blanco')

SCULPTURAL METAL

In summer, display larger cacti and succulents in a sunny, sheltered spot outdoors. The sculptural forms of opuntia, agave, and the treelike aeonium create a modern feel, especially in metal containers.

MULCHES

As well as being ornamental, using a free-draining mulch around succulents and alpines helps to keep the foliage and stem base dry, preventing rotting.

SLATE

Slate shards work well with mountain-loving alpines. Used edge-up, they create interesting texture.

GRAVEL

Fine gravel, pebbles, or stone chips set off succulents like this *Haworthia* perfectly.

BLUE GLASS

Emphasize the surreal shapes of plants using a contemporary mulch of glass chips.

Patio planting

YOU WILL NEED

Heavy-duty gardening gloves
and protective goggles

Mallet and chisel

Multi-purpose compost with added
soil-based compost

Slow-release fertilizer granules

Compost scoop or trowel

Plant of your choice (*Phormium*
'Evening Glow' shown here)

Decorative pebbles to finish

Laying concrete paving slabs is a practical and economical way of creating a level surface in a garden, but it is not always the most attractive solution. One quick way of adding some glamour and color to a dull patio is to remove a slab and plant in the space instead.

You can use different plants to suit the conditions in your garden, including shade. As well as color, evergreen interest, or fragrance, you might want the plant to add height or partially screen an area. In this case you could use a well-behaved columnar bamboo like *Fargesia murielae* 'Simba' or black bamboo (*Phyllostachys nigra*).

Here, we have used the deep pink *Phormium* 'Evening Glow'. This adds flair and is also low maintenance and will relish the warm micro-climate and shelter close to the house.

1 Pick your spot

Choose the best place to plant—make sure the location suits your plant's needs in terms of sun, shelter, etc. A slab at the edge of the patio is easier to remove than one surrounded by others on all sides.

2 Loosening the slab

First put on heavy-duty gloves and goggles to protect yourself from flying bits of concrete. Position the chisel in the cement around the slab, and hammer it in. Work around the slab to loosen the seal.

3 Clearing the planting area

Once you have loosened the seal, use the chisel to pry the slab up, lifting the stone away carefully. Once the slab is removed, dig out any stones, sand, or cement that remain.

4 Prepare the soil

Remove soil from the hole to the depth of the plant's pot, and roughly turn over the soil underneath. Fill the hole with compost that has been pre-mixed with fertilizer granules.

5 Plant up

Push the potted plant into the compost to make a planting hole, and check that the planting level is right. Remove the pot, carefully tease out the roots, place the plant in the hole, and backfill with compost.

6 Finishing touch

Gently firm around the base of the plant, then, once the soil surface is level, place decorative pebbles around the base. Pack them tightly to prevent weeds from growing, but do not damage the plant.

Hanging basket care

Hanging baskets can be troublesome to maintain, but with careful planning when preparing and planting baskets, and the use of labor-saving products, they can flourish.

TOP TIPS

Beautifully luxuriant basket displays require some regular care to stay their best. Start with as big a basket as you can manage; 14–16in (35–40cm) is ideal. Plant up with a good quality container compost that has added moisture-holding compounds and slow-release fertilizer. Then follow these tips.

WATERING
Install an automatic irrigation kit (see pp.176–177), or water 16-in (40-cm) baskets every two days using a lance attachment.

FEEDING
Add slow-release fertilizer at planting time. In midsummer, start adding liquid feed every two weeks for flowering plants.

DEADHEADING
Regularly remove faded flowers and yellowing leaves to keep plants from producing new blooms and to reduce disease.

PULLEY SYSTEM

Access for tending hanging baskets can be a problem, but installing a pulley device makes light work of watering and deadheading. The device is attached to the wall bracket and then to the basket hooks on the other end. You can pull the basket down to a comfortable working height, and then guide it back up to its original position.

UP (LEFT)
Hang the basket at a height where you can reach the base.

DOWN (RIGHT)
The basket pulls down so you can water, feed, and deadhead your plants with ease.

PERFECT PLANTS

If you can't water baskets regularly or install irrigation, use bright heat- and drought-tolerant plants. To maintain a basket's good looks, use resilient plants, avoiding drought-sensitive lobelia, petunia, and impatiens.

DROUGHT-TOLERANT

These plants are survivors. Plant them with loam-based compost and gel crystals.

* Kingfisher daisy (*Felicia amelloides*)
* Livingstone daisy (*Dorotheanthus bellidiformis*)
* Parrot's bill (*Lotus berthelotii*)
* *Rhodanthemum hosmariense*
* *Sedum lineare* 'Variegatum'
* Sun plant (*Portulaca grandiflora*)
* Zonal or trailing geranium (*Pelargonium*)

SPEEDY RECOVERY

These flowers can recover from a few missed waterings—but do not let them dry out too badly.

* *Begonia semperflorens*
* *Bidens ferulifolia*
* *Diascia*
* French marigold (*Tagetes*)
* *Nemesia* (e.g. Maritana Series)
* *Scaevola aemula*
* *Brachyscome multifida*
* Trailing verbena (*Verbena* Tapien Series)

FOLIAGE FALLBACK

Basket flowers often bloom in phases, so add variegated and colored foliage plants too.

* *Dichondra* 'Silver Falls'
* English ivy (*Hedera helix*)
* Golden creeping Jenny (*Lysimachia nummularia* 'Aurea')
* *Helichrysum petiolare*
* *Lysimachia congestiflora* 'Outback Sunset'
* Morning glory (*Ipomoea*)
* Trailing nepeta (*Glechoma hederacea* 'Variegata')

WATERING TIPS

Using simple techniques when making up your basket means that plants are far less likely to dry out. Try a waterproof liner that has drainage holes a third of the way up from the base, or see right.

RESERVOIR
Place a plastic pot saucer or even an old ceramic one in the basket base.

GEL CRYSTALS
Following packet instructions, add gel crystals to compost.

◑ EMERGENCY RESCUE

Plunge a wilted basket in a bowl or sink of water overnight. It may float and need holding down initially. After recovery, cut out any dead stems, and deadhead spent blooms.

Summer basket

YOU WILL NEED

16in (40cm) basket with coir liner

Black plastic sheeting and scissors

Multi-purpose potting compost with added soil-based compost

Slow-release fertilizer granules and water-retaining gel crystals

1 x bedding dahlia, 3 x dwarf Marguerite daisies, 3 x *Petunia* Surfinia, 4 x *Brachyscome multifida*, 3 x variegated *Helichrysum*

Oyster shell (pictured) or gravel mulch

A single basket of bright flowers and colorful foliage acts as a cheerful welcome sign beside the front door. Baskets can brighten up any patch of bare wall and are particularly welcome around a patio or deck, especially if there is no room beside your seating area for borders in which you can grow colorful climbers or wall-trained shrubs.

Try fixing several baskets at different heights, making sure you can reach to water them. A long-lance fitting on your hose is useful when watering baskets and other hard-to-reach places.

For ease of planting and after-care, choose a pre-lined basket, or add your own liner as shown here. A large 16in (40cm) basket will retain moisture better than a smaller basket.

1 Prepare the liner
Unhook one of the basket's chains to make planting easier. Cut a large circle of black plastic sheeting to act as a reservoir, and place it in the bottom of the liner.

2 Add fertilizer
Following the packet instructions, add slow-release fertilizer granules to the potting mix. Partially fill the basket with the compost, then add water-retaining gel crystals. Mix in well.

3 Position the centerpiece
After thoroughly soaking the plants in a bucket, set the dahlia in the middle—this has the largest blooms and will act as an eye-catching centerpiece.

4 Plant and mulch
Add daisies and petunias next, and set trailing plants—in this case the helichrysum—around the basket rim. Fill around the root balls with more potting mix, water, then finish with the mulch.

5 Finished
Reattach the chains, and select the side of the basket you would like facing forward before hanging. Hang on a sturdy bracket or hook in a sunny spot.

TIMELY ADVICE

❋ **Deadhead** Use your fingers or scissors to nip off any faded blooms and yellowing leaves. This encourages repeat-flowering and limits disease.

❋ **Water regularly** Do this even if it seems to be raining constantly; every other day should be enough for large hanging baskets.

❋ **Top-off feed** Flowers benefit from additional liquid feeding, especially in late summer. Pick a feed that's suitable for use with bedding plants in containers.

❋ **Trim excess foliage** Use scissors or shears to get rid of any excess foliage and to keep the basket looking well-balanced.

DIY patio canopy

YOU WILL NEED

Fabric (width of pergola x 1½ times length)

Cordless drill and drill bit

Vine eyes and screwdriver

Thick galvanized training wire

Pliers or wire cutters

Iron-on hem tape

Plastic clothespins and tablecloth weights

While you are waiting for climbers to cover a pergola, you can create instant privacy with fabric. A billowing "ceiling" of translucent cotton or muslin adds a wonderful "Arabian Nights" feel to the summer patio. People looking down into the garden from surrounding houses won't be able to see through, but the area remains light and airy. Cotton sheeting is ideal (you may even be able to recycle old bed sheets) but any light, quick-drying fabric, such as muslin, will do: look for inexpensive remnants in fabric stores.

Vine eyes are sold in garden centers or home stores alongside training wire and plant supports.

1 Drill pilot holes

Decide where the support wires will run. Ideally they should lie beneath the cross pieces of the pergola. Drill pilot holes, selecting a drill bit that is slightly smaller than the shaft of the vine eye.

2 Screw in vine eyes

Vine eyes and training wire are used to create supports for climbing plants and wall-trained fruit, but they're ideal here too. Insert the vine eyes in the pilot holes, and tighten with a screwdriver as shown.

3 Thread the wire

Thread wire through the eye, leaving enough spare wire with which to fasten off. Stretch the wire across to the eye on the other side, pulling it taut and twisting the ends around with pliers to secure.

4 Prepare the fabric

On the fabric, turn over any edges that can fray, and finish with iron-on hem tape. This method is much quicker than sewing.

5 Peg in place

Drape the fabric over the wires, spreading it out to create even "billows." Hold in place using clothespins.

6 Add weights

Hanging tablecloth weights—available from fabric stores—from the four corners of the canopy stops the material from flipping back over the wires in the breeze.

Providing quick privacy

In order to feel comfortable sitting and eating outdoors in your own garden, you need to know that there are places where you can relax without being watched by neighbors or passersby. Sometimes all that is required is a strategically placed tree. Alternatively, there are a number of easy solutions, some seasonal, others permanent.

 ## QUICK SCREENS

You can create privacy quickly and inexpensively using plants and temporary frames. Some have the bonus of adding color and fragrance to the terrace or may be dual purpose, screening the patio with an edible crop like runner beans. Annual flowering climbers such as Canary creeper (*Tropaeolum peregrinum*) are particularly speedy.

TOMATO PLANTERS

Choosing a sunny, sheltered spot, plant a line of cordon tomatoes, acclimatized to outdoor conditions, about 18in (45cm) apart. Good varieties include 'Gardener's Delight' and 'Sweet 100'. Deep, heavy troughs provide more stability and better growing conditions than growing bags. Insert expanding trellis and bamboo poles for support. Tie new growth in regularly.

FLOWER LINE

A row of identically planted containers on top of a retaining wall creates an informal flowering hedge.

POTS ON WHEELS

Bamboos like *Phyllostachys aurea* and *Fargesia nitida* in wheeled troughs or pots provide handy, mobile screens.

 ## MAKE IT

❋ **Grow seedlings** Sow hardy annual sweet peas on a light window ledge in spring (use deep, root-trainer units), or buy ready-grown plants already acclimatized to outdoor conditions.

❋ **Make a bamboo frame** Prepare some ground next to paving and add homemade compost to retain moisture. Erect the frame, plant, and then water.

BRIGHT IDEAS

Screening solutions can make permanent patio or terrace features and be highly decorative as well as functional. The ideas below show how you can create privacy without making an area feel dark or cut off from the rest of the garden.

COLORFUL SAILS

Once you had to order pull-out triangular awnings from sail makers, but white or colored treated-fabric patio sails are now widely available for purchase in garden centers and online.

STAINED GLASS PANELS

This screen is made from a number of stained glass strips, but you could purchase old stained glass windows from salvage yards to incorporate into a conventional trellis partition.

LIGHT SCREENS

Made from translucent plastic sheeting and wood, these panels are perfect for creating a roomlike quality, especially when incorporated into a pergola. Because they let in so much light, you can use them as dividers in shady courtyards.

FENCE PORTHOLES

Some trellis and fence manufacturers make panels with windowlike openings that screen effectively but allow glimpsed views through to the garden or landscape beyond. Make your own by cutting a rectangular window in trellis and framing it with wood.

Patio cleaning

After a long, wet winter the patio can look a little worse for wear, but in no time at all you can have it clean and fresh and ready for long summer days outside. Dirt, moss, and algae can take up residence on pots, garden furniture, and paving over the winter. This not only looks bad but can also make surfaces slippery and dangerous to walk on. As well as making the patio a more pleasant place to sit, a spring cleaning will lengthen the life of garden accessories.

☸ PRESSURE WASH THE PATIO

Using a hard-bristled broom, first sweep away the surface debris and any loose muck. Connect the pressure hose to the tap and then to the electrical power point, and methodically work your way across the paving. Be careful not to waste water or overdo the pressure washing; powerful jets can erode mortar and remove some paving surfaces.

☽ CLEANING POTS

The weathered look on terra-cotta pots can look charming, but they can be cleaned up if you prefer. Algae builds up over time in damp conditions, and needs elbow grease to remove it. Go over the pot with a stiff brush, then scrub using hot soapy water. A dash of lemon juice or vinegar in the water can make the job a little easier.

INSTANT IMPACT <<

❋ **Revitalize pots** For a fresh look in minutes, remove tired old plants from pots, and cover the exposed soil with gravel, pebbles, or slate. Clear away any unwanted pots.

❋ **Soften up** Closed umbrellas always look sad and dejected, so open them up. For more color,

buy vibrant seat covers, and place matching lanterns on the table.

❋ **Centerpiece** A nice pot of low-growing herbs or flowers adds a lovely touch to the table.

❋ **Clear clutter** A neatened patio instantly looks better, so clear as you go for a clutter-free look.

◑ CLEANING UPHOLSTERY

If you cannot remove your outdoor seat covers for washing, or need to clean your parasol, gently dab any marks on the material with a soft cloth and a spray of mild detergent and warm water.

◑ PILLOWS

Throw pillows can turn an exterior space into a cozy outdoor room. A few scattered on garden chairs, sofas, or even on the floor soften hard landscaping and add color on a dull day. Many types of inexpensive pillows are available—even practical waterproof kinds.

◑ CLEAN FURNITURE

Wooden garden furniture can turn a depressing shade of gray over winter. A good scrub using a scouring pad and warm soapy water should remove the ingrained dirt and restore the wood's natural color.

◑ OIL WOOD

Apply teak oil to protect wood from rot and mildew and improve its look. Pour oil into a jar, and apply evenly to dry, prepared wood with a clean paintbrush. Consider leaving oak bare to weather naturally.

≫ IF YOU HAVE MORE TIME

❊ **Clear away weeds** The gaps between paving slabs offer a tempting home to weeds and moss. You can apply special path weedkiller, but if you are an organic gardener, use a trowel to scrape out unwelcome plants.

❊ **Brighten up woodwork** If you have fencing or trellis around your patio, give it a good brush down to remove any dirt, then apply a new coat of woodstain, or perhaps even a colored wood paint to brighten up the area.

Mosaic tile

Express your artistic side with this simple garden craft project. It is easy to make once you have gotten everything together that you need. The beauty of the basic grid design used here is that it is very versatile; you can arrange the beads symmetrically in rows or blocks, or, as in this example, asymmetrically.

Use this project idea to decorate a paving slab or tile that is already part of a paved area, or apply it to a spare slab, and use it to enhance potted plant arrangements. If you have a patio made of gravel or slate, set it in the middle to create an eye-catching centerpiece. The tile could also be mounted on a wall or used to decorate the side of a raised bed with the right fixings.

Position the slab somewhere that has some frost protection since this will help prevent the beads from loosening.

1 Apply grout to the tile
Use the flexible grout spreader to apply an even layer of grout to the slab or tile. You need a sufficiently thick layer to embed the beads to half their thickness.

2 Mark out the pattern
Use a nail or pencil to score a grid pattern of equal squares, measuring first to ensure equal spacing between the vertical and horizontal lines.

3 Start to apply the beads
Beginning at the center with a square of blue beads, build up the pattern around it using green beads. At this stage only press the beads in lightly to position them.

BRIGHT IDEAS

❊ **Slate mosaic** Arrange slender slate shards, selected from a bag of slate chips, to create a fluid design. Place the shards edge-on into a fairly thick layer of grout. Slate shards will suit a simple spiral or starburst design.

❊ **Mirrored tile** Decorate a slate roof tile by gluing or cementing on a design made from shards of broken CDs or mirror tiles. Protect your eyes with goggles when cutting these materials. Use the nail holes in the roof tile to hang it on the wall.

❊ **Store-bought mosaic** Cut sheets of mosaic wall tiles into blocks and strips, and stick them onto a slab or tile using tile adhesive. Grout between the tiles, and remove any excess with an old cloth.

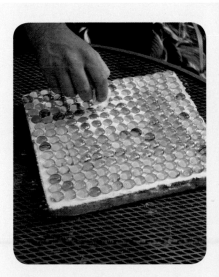

4 Complete the design

Add more beads, following the scored guides. When finished, press the beads down. Then, when almost dry, gently wipe away any excess grout with an old cloth.

Beautiful borders

With a little planning you can create colorful borders of shrubs, perennials, and climbers that will keep their good looks through all four seasons. And whether you lean toward English cottage-garden charm or prefer a more contemporary look, you can even overcome tricky conditions by knowing which are the right plants to use. Plus, there are quick and easy ways to revitalize flagging displays and create a border from scratch.

Spring makeover

Carry out your makeover in stages using the weather and signs of new growth as your guide. Some jobs like mulching, or pruning tough deciduous shrubs like bush roses, can be done very early on provided it isn't frosty.

⊕ PRUNING

Hard prune shrubs that flower mid- to late summer such as bush roses, butterfly bush (*Buddleja davidii*), mallow (*Lavatera*) and *Hydrangea paniculata*, but don't prune *Hydrangea macrophylla*. Hard prune colored-stem dogwoods, brambles (see pp.182–183), and gold-leaf spireas.
In late winter, prune *Clematis viticella* and *Clematis texensis*. Cut 12in (30cm) from the ground, above a pair of strong buds.

⊕ WEEDING

Pull out or spray off (using glyphosate-based ready-mixed weedkiller spray) the rash of annual weed seedlings that appears as the weather warms. Getting a head start now will save work later. Fork out perennial weed roots. For problem weeds, spray with glyphosate.

⊕ FEED THE SOIL

Apply bulky organic matter such as well-rotted manure, spent mushroom compost, or homemade compost as a mulch in late winter or early spring before perennials begin to grow in earnest. Leave a gap around the neck of plants to protect the stems.

INSTANT IMPACT ‹‹

❋ **Cut back or pull away dead stems** Tidy flower stems and seed pods left on plants for winter interest, and remove dead leaves on evergreen perennials such as *Bergenia*. With deciduous grasses, wait until new growth emerges before pulling dead leaves off.

❋ **Prune penstemons** Cut back to just above where new leafy shoots appear in the bottom half of the plant.

❋ **Plant potted spring bulbs** Keep the spring bulbs in their pots, and plant directly into your border. Disguise the top of the pot with soil.

🕐 TIE-IN NEW PLANTS
New growth on climbers and wall shrubs is vulnerable to weather damage. Tie in regularly to support wires or a trellis, guiding stems to cover areas evenly.

🕐 DEADHEAD BULBS
Remove fading blooms and seed pods of larger headed bulbs like daffodils and tulips. Leave the stems and foliage to die down naturally for 6–8 weeks to allow the new bulb, containing next year's flowers, to develop. Feed with liquid tomato fertilizer.

🕐 ADD SUPPORTS
Push in plant supports early on so that the emerging growth camouflages the structure. Try supports like pea sticks, available from garden centers, for supporting tall perennials like delphiniums.

🕐 DIVIDE PLANTS
Lift and divide perennials to keep plants vigorous and flowering strongly. Discard old, non-productive parts. Replant in well-cultivated soil, adding a top dressing of general fertilizer to kick-start growth.

>> IF YOU HAVE MORE TIME

❋ **Sow hardy annuals** Fill gaps with quick-to-flower hardy annuals like pot marigold and Shirley poppy, sowing in drills within raked-over patches to make weed seedling detection easier.

❋ **Plant summer bulbs** For exotic-looking summer blooms, plant hardy bulbs like lilies or pot-grown ornamental onions (*Allium*).

Late spring border

This design of bulbs, wallflowers, and blossoming shrubs is bursting with color, not to mention fragrance. The abundant flowers and bright fresh foliage are an expression of the weather warming. Even if you didn't plant your bulbs last fall, you can still reproduce this cheerful prelude to summer using plants purchased in bud from garden centers.

COOL HUES
The North American camas (*Camassia quamash*) is a bulb that bridges the gap between spring and summer, enjoying the same cool conditions as deciduous azalea.

GET THE LOOK

On acid soil (pH below 7, see p.8), plant one deciduous azalea. Dig in moisture-retentive organic matter beforehand if the soil is very light. For neutral to alkaline soils, plant *Kerria japonica* 'Pleniflora' (back of border). Plant a grouping of three pots of camas in front. Finish with a foreground of five pots of wallflowers in bud. Interplant with five pots of tulips such as 'Strong Gold' or 'Golden Apeldoorn'.

TULIPOMANIA
Triumph group tulips like 'Strong Gold' (pictured) have long stems and weather-resilient blooms that work well with taller bedding—like wallflowers and forget-me-nots.

BEDDING TIME
Fragrant annual wallflowers (*Erysimum cheiri*) attract early butterflies and bees. Traditionally planted in the fall, buy potted plants in the spring for instant results.

BLOOMS
The deciduous woodland azalea *Rhododendron luteum* has a powerful perfume. It thrives in well-mulched, moisture-retentive, acidic soil.

FINISHING TOUCHES

This design thrives in the sun, although partial shade is sufficient. The azalea and camas enjoy dappled shade from overhanging trees.

❋ **Tulip medley** Consider blending other tulips into your design. Ones with overlapping flowering periods extend the display. Here, two-tone orange-red and yellow tulips add a luxurious touch and tie the colors together. If planting bulbs in fall, plant 9in (23cm) deep to increase chances of successful flowering in subsequent years.

❋ **Bridging the seasons** Plant ornamental onion, *Allium hollandicum* 'Purple Sensation' (pictured in bud) to follow on from the tulips.

MORE PLANT OPTIONS

COOL HUES *Brunnera macrophylla;* Canterbury bells (*Campanula medium*) purple-blue or white types; English bluebell (*Hyacinthoides non-scripta*); honesty (*Lunaria annua* and the white *Lunaria annua* var. *albiflora*); white foxglove (*Digitalis purpurea* f. *albiflora*)

TULIPOMANIA *Tulipa* 'Ballerina' (orange); *Tulipa* 'Queen of Night' (dark maroon); *Tulipa* 'Queen of Sheba' (orange-red with yellow petal margins); *Tulipa* 'Striped Bellona' (yellow petals, feathered red)

BEDDING TIME Drumstick primula (*Primula denticulata*); forget-me-not (*Myosotis sylvatica*); perennial wallflower (*Erysimum* 'Constant Cheer'); polyanthus cultivars

BLOOMS *Chaenomeles* x *superba* cultivars; *Exochorda* x *macrantha* 'The Bride'; flowering currant (*Ribes sanguineum* cultivars and *Ribes odoratum*); *Kerria japonica* 'Pleniflora'; *Viburnum* x *burkwoodii*; *Viburnum* x *carlcephalum*

Summer makeover

At this time of year mixed borders benefit from regular "housekeeping" to encourage continued flowering and to keep on top of potential problems caused by pests, lack of rain, and overzealous growth of both ornamentals and weeds.

◐ KEEP ALLIUM HEADS

Early summer flowering ornamental onions, like *Allium hollandicum* 'Purple Sensation' and the large starry globes of *Allium cristophii*, produce long-lasting, architectural seedheads, so don't deadhead.

◑ TIE-IN CLEMATIS

By midsummer climbers and wall shrubs have often produced a profusion of new stems. Guide shoots in the right direction, and tie in to supports early to prevent them from latching on to nearby plants or forming a dense, tangled mass.

◑ STOP SEEDING PROBLEMS

Although self-seeding by some plants is welcome, others, like lady's mantle (*Alchemilla mollis*), set so much they become weedlike. Prevent this by cutting them to ground level after flowering, then feed and water for fresh foliage.

INSTANT IMPACT ≪

- ❋ **Trim lawn edges** Neatening lawn edges with lawn shears or electric trimmers, and at the same time weeding the border margins, will make your borders look even more attractive.

- ❋ **Top off ornamental bark mulch** Mulches will reduce moisture loss and complete the look.

- ❋ **Remove flowering weeds** If you are quick to pull out or dig up flowering weeds before they set seed, it will save you a lot of work later. Also remove excess seedlings of ornamentals.

- ❋ **Prune early-flowering shrubs** (see pp.186–187)

🕐 PEST PATROL

Rub off aphids from shoot tips and flower buds. Handpick caterpillars, and go on flashlight patrols for slugs and snails. Destroy lily beetles (pictured) and vine weevil adults (use biological control for larvae).

🕐 DEADHEAD

Remove faded flowers of annuals and tender perennials using thumb and forefinger or flower scissors. For tougher stems like roses, use shears, cutting just above a bud.

🕐 WATER WISE

Restrict watering to recent plantings, including ones put in the previous fall through to spring, because these might not have a big enough root system yet to deal with summer dryness. Water early or late in the day to avoid excess evaporation.

🕐 CUT-AND-COME-AGAIN

To encourage more flowers, cut off the faded flower stems of cranesbill geraniums, and remove the main flower spike of lupines, delphiniums, bellflowers, and verbascums near the base, just above a bud.

≫ IF YOU HAVE MORE TIME

❋ **Cut back foliage shrubs** Deciduous shrubs grown for foliage effect often grow out of proportion. Trim to restore balance and discourage legginess. Also prune or reshape evergreens.

❋ **Rejuvenate perennials** Some perennials e.g. catmint (*Nepeta x faassenii*) and *Lamium maculatum* form blooms in flushes if cut back after flowering. Feed and water to promote regrowth.

Summer border

This bright but cool design has tons of style. For a similar feel, combine the highlighted plants, or if you have more space, choose from the list opposite. All thrive in sun.

 **GET THE LOOK**

Zigzag 5–7 *Knautia* 'Melton Pastels' (mid- to back border). Weave in three pots of *Nectaroscordum*. In the foreground, plant a meandering line of five red valerian (*Centranthus ruber* 'Albus'). Among these dot three *Salvia* 'Mainacht' and three lady's mantle.

LIVING SCULPTURE

An unexpected bonus of *Nectaroscordum siculum* is that after the pendulous flowers have faded, striking seedheads form, reminiscent of fairytale castles. Buy in bloom, or plant bulbs in the fall.

TALL STORY

Floating above the other perennials, *Knautia* 'Melton Pastels' has airy, branched stems of small rounded blooms, a magnet for bees and butterflies. Deadhead regularly.

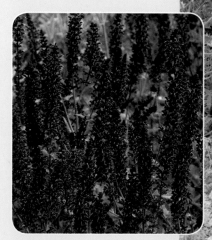

REPEAT PERFORMERS

Many of the plants suggested for this project keep flowering for months, and the white type of red valerian (*Centranthus ruber* 'Albus') is no exception.

SOFT FOIL

Show off the colors and forms of bold perennials using the neutral, 'soft focus' backdrop of the low-growing lady's mantle (*Alchemilla mollis*).

SOLID COLOR

You won't need many *Salvia* 'Mainacht' to light up a design. The rich flowers add depth and contrast among the softer pastel shades.

FINISHING TOUCHES

The contemporary feel here is mostly due to the restricted palette of bright pinks and purples, freshened with white, yellow, and lime green.

❋ **Repeating theme** Using a structure of the same three or four plants into which others are dotted helps to hold the border together aesthetically. Natural-looking layering works better here than a rigid height-graded scheme of largest at the back, shortest at the front.

❋ **Plain backdrop** A clipped yew hedge provides a plain backdrop that helps the flowers to stand out. A treated wall or stained fence would also work.

❋ **Winding path** To achieve this carefree look, lay a wide pathway so that there is room for plants to flow over and soften the edges.

MORE PLANT OPTIONS

LIVING SCULPTURE *Acanthus spinosus*; *Allium hollandicum* 'Purple Sensation'; cardoon (*Cynara cardunculus*); *Eryngium alpinum* 'Blue Star'); daylily (*Hemerocallis*); *Iris* 'Jane Phillips'

TALL STORY 'Black' hollyhock (*Alcea rosea* 'Nigra'); Japanese anemone (*Anemone* x *hybrida* 'Honorine Jobert'); *Verbascum* 'Gainsborough'; *Perovskia* 'Blue Spire'; *Verbena bonariensis*

REPEAT PERFORMERS Craneshill (*Geranium* Rozanne); *Geum* 'Lady Stratheden'; *Scabiosa caucasica* 'Clive Greaves'; *Veronica spicata*

SOFT FOIL *Artemisia absinthium* 'Lambrook Silver'; catmint (*Nepeta* x *faassenii*); golden marjoram (*Origanum vulgare* 'Aureum')

SOLID COLOR Cranesbill (*Geranium* 'Dragon Heart'); *Lychnis coronaria* Atrosanguinea Group; *Salvia verticillata* 'Purple Rain'; *Achillea* 'Moonshine'

Instant color lift

Create instant color impact and an exotic look to your borders by using flowering plants and foliage like theatrical props. Large, statuesque plants such as cannas, or the Ethiopian banana plant (*Ensete ventricosum* 'Maurelii', shown right) can be placed outdoors for the summer using the surrounding border plants to camouflage the pot. Black plastic pots are almost invisible in this situation and are ideal for temporary highlights such as lilies.

⏱ PLUNGE PLANTING

Tender perennials and bulbs that require overwintering in a frost-free place make ideal candidates for "plunge planting." After gradually acclimatizing plants that have been nurtured under cover, usually for a period of two to three weeks, simply dig a hole, and place the plant, still in its pot, within it. This gives the impression that the plant is growing in the border and allows you to add color wherever you need it. Lift in the fall for winter protection.

DAHLIAS
Plant pots with dahlia tubers like 'Bishop of Llandaff' (pictured) in the spring. Move them to bigger pots as they grow, then, as they start to bloom, "plunge" them, in their pots, into the beds.

BRIGHT IDEAS

Create a luxuriant oasis in summer by using tender house- and sunroom plants that enjoy a few months outside before returning to their usual spot. Sow or buy tropical-looking annual climbers for quick blooms at eye level, and in spring add instant color with pots of bulbs.

SPRING SPLASH

Buy potted bulbs in spring, or plant bulbs in fall in perforated aquatic baskets, adding color where needed. Plant permanently, or plunge baskets for easy lifting later.

* *Fritillaria imperialis* cultivars
* *Hyacinthus orientalis* 'Delft Blue'
* *Hyacinthus orientalis* 'Gypsy Queen'
* *Narcissus* 'Jetfire'
* *Narcissus* 'Juanita'
* *Tulipa* 'Flaming Parrot'
* *Tulipa* 'Orange Emperor'
* *Tulipa* 'Red Riding Hood'
* *Tulipa* 'West Point'

CLIMBER HIGHLIGHTS

Some flamboyant annual climbers, like this morning glory, are actually tender perennials. All grow rapidly up stakes, obelisks, or trellis, making their mark in a sheltered patio bed or main border.

* *Cobaea scandens*
* *Eccremocarpus scaber*
* *Gloriosa superba* 'Rothschildiana'
* *Ipomoea lobata*
* *Ipomoea purpurea* 'Purple Haze'
* *Rhodochiton atrosanguineus*
* *Thunbergia alata* 'African Sunset'
* *Tropaeolum majus* 'Climbing Mixed'
* *Tropaeolum peregrinum*

INSIDE OUT

Move sunroom plants outside once the nights begin to warm up to create an exotic feel outdoors. Use wheeled bases for unwieldy, larger pots and containers.

* *Abutilon* 'Canary Bird'
* *Abutilon* 'Kentish Belle'
* *Abutilon megapotamicum*
* *Cordyline australis* 'Torbay Dazzler'
* *Hibiscus rosa-sinensis*
* Kumquat (*Fortunella margarita*)
* Mandarin (*Citrus reticulata*)
* *Plumbago auriculata*
* *Tibouchina urvilleana*

Planting a tree

PLANT Mid-spring to fall

YOU WILL NEED
Spade and fork
Tree in pot (Hawthorn (*Crataegus*) shown)
Bamboo pole or similar
Multi-purpose compost with added soil-based compost
Tree stake and flexible tree tie with spacer
Mallet
Chipped bark mulch

To give your tree the best start in life, it is worth making sure it is planted correctly. It is not a difficult or time-consuming job and will pay dividends in the long term. The key considerations are providing the right conditions, making sure the roots have plenty of room to establish themselves, and protecting the tree from adverse weather or animal damage that may hinder its growth.

Container-grown trees are best planted between mid-spring and fall, but the less expensive bare-root trees can be planted in winter. This must be done right after purchase, and they should be planted in the same way as container-grown trees.

All trees need deep, well-drained soil with ground around it that is plant-free, to reduce competition.

Trees will provide a long-term feature in the garden, but in

1 Prepare the planting hole
Position the tree where you would like it to be, then dig a hole about three times the diameter of the pot and one and a half times the depth of the root ball. Put a layer of well-rotted manure in the hole.

2 Check the level
Plant the tree at the level it was in the pot for the best start. Place the pot in the hole, and lay a pole across it to check the depth. Pierce the sides of the hole with a fork to encourage a stronger root system.

3 Prepare the tree
Carefully remove the tree from its pot—this is best done by laying the plant on its side first. Gently tease out the roots, being careful not to break up the root ball in the process.

order to keep them healthy, they need after-care. Young trees, like any new plants, must be regularly watered until established, but they also require protection against adverse weather conditions. Stakes prevent trees from being blown over or the stems from snapping in high winds, while some frost-tender species may need covering with fabric when frost is forecast. Country gardeners may also need to protect young stems against bark-stripping pests like deer or rabbits.

TIMELY ADVICE

❋ **Water well** Let the potted tree stand in a bucket of water for 1–2 hours prior to planting, then water it thoroughly after planting. It is essential to water regularly while the tree is establishing itself, particularly in hot, dry weather.

❋ **Protect the trunk** If you have animal visitors to your garden such as rabbits, it is advisable to protect the young bark by covering it with a layer of chicken wire, plastic netting, or a spiral tree guard.

❋ **Check stakes** Check the tree stake to see if it is securely anchored in the ground and has not shifted after periods of bad weather or high winds. If so, hammer it back into place immediately. After two or three years the tree should be sufficiently established for the stake to be removed.

4 Planting
Position the tree in the hole so its best side is on view. Backfill around the tree with multi-purpose compost and the topsoil you removed earlier. Firm the soil down gently, ensuring the tree is upright.

5 Stake and secure
Young trees need staking to protect them from wind damage. Position the stake at a 45° angle, hammer into the ground, then attach to the tree with a tie. Water well, then mulch with chipped bark.

Fall border

The ideal design is one that looks good for 12 months but peaks at a particular time. With the right combination of plants, including ones that will improve with age, a border can start to come alive as summer wanes and winter approaches. Plant your fall display where it can be appreciated from indoors.

GET THE LOOK

After thorough soil preparation (see pp.8–9), follow this planting design for a stunning fall border. At the back of the border, put in one purple moor grass (*Molinia caerulea* subsp. *arundinacea*). In front and around this, plant a shallow 'V' of 3–5 *Sedum* 'Herbstfreude'. To one side, at the front of the border, plant a block of five *Erica* x *darleyensis* 'Kramer's Rote', and to the other side plant 1–3 specimens of *Pennisetum orientale*.

GOLDEN FOUNTAIN
There are numerous varieties of purple moor grass (*Molinia caerulea* subsp. *arundinacea*), and this one, 'Zuneigung', creates a shimmering focal point in low fall light.

LATE BLOOMER
The butterfly magnet *Sedum* 'Herbstfreude' has apple-green flower buds in the summer that gradually darken to brick pink and then finally to a deep mahogany.

SOFT TOUCH
The fluffy-headed Asian fountain grass (*Pennisetum orientale*) is too tempting to pass by without touching. Place at the front of the border or overhanging a pathway.

COLOR CARPET
The heath *Erica* x *darleyensis* 'Darley Dale' is lime-tolerant, flowering from winter to spring. 'Kramer's Rote' buds in fall and blooms in early winter.

FINISHING TOUCHES

A mulch of ornamental bark after planting controls weed growth. Follow the tips below, and your fall border will be easy to keep.

※ **Spring groom** Once new leaves start to emerge in spring, cut clumps back to around 3in (7.5cm) above ground. Protect *Pennisetum* roots with a dry bark mulch.

※ **Heather trim** After flowering in spring, cut back, removing old flower spikes. This keeps plants compact.

※ **Sedum chop** Every couple of years in spring, lift and divide clumps, discarding old centers and splitting to keep plants youthful. This keeps flower stems from collapsing.

※ **Shrub foil** Plant fall- and winter-flowering evergreens like *Viburnum tinus* 'Eve Price' and *Camellia sasanqua* cultivars (need acid soil) to form a backdrop.

MORE PLANT OPTIONS

GOLDEN FOUNTAIN *Miscanthus sinensis* 'Kleine Fontäne'; *Stipa calamagrostis*; *Stipa gigantea*; tufted hair grass (*Deschampsia cespitosa* 'Goldgehänge')

LATE BLOOMER *Helenium* cultivars; Japanese anemone (*Anemone* x *hybrida* cultivars); Michaelmas daisy (*Aster novi-belgii*) and *Aster frikartii* 'Mönch'; *Penstemon* 'Blackbird'; Russian sage (*Perovskia* 'Blue Spire')

SOFT TOUCH *Pennisetum alopecuroides* cultivars (hardier than *Pennisetum orientale*), e.g. 'Cassian's Choice' and 'Hameln'; *Stipa tenuissima*

COLOR CARPET Fall-flowering heaths and heathers, e.g. *Calluna vulgaris* and *Erica cinerea* cultivars (both of which need acid soil); hardy plumbago (*Ceratostigma plumbaginoides*)

Winter border

Contrasting form and texture are important elements in designing a border for winter interest. In this planting scheme, foliage plays a key role, with rounded shapes of *Bergenia* leaves contrasting with the linear quality of dogwood (*Cornus*) stems. If you have room, using bold swathes of the same plant looks dramatic even if the subject matter is fairly simple.

🕐 GET THE LOOK

This design thrives on well-drained but moisture-retentive soil in sun. The hellebore leaves provide a striking contrast to the red stems of the dogwoods (*Cornus*). When these shrubs come into leaf, the hellebores will continue to thrive in the partial shade. Plant three *Cornus* in a loose group at the back with five hellebores (*Helleborus foetidus*) at their base. Add a cluster of 3–5 *Bergenia* in the foreground to one side, and finish on the other side with 5–7 heathers.

HARDY BLOOMERS
The weather-resistant heather *Erica* x *darleyensis* 'Arthur Johnson' blooms from early winter into spring. Its honey-scented flowers attract early insects.

EVERGREEN GLOSS
Spring-flowering *Bergenia* 'Bressingham Ruby' has glossy evergreen leaves that develop into shades of red and maroon as the temperatures drop.

GLOWING STEMS
These shiny red dogwoods (*Cornus alba* 'Sibirica') seem to gleam in low winter sunlight. Ring them with yellow- or white-stemmed alternatives.

FLORAL SCULPTURE
In late spring the hellebore's deep green palmate foliage is joined by the sculpted apple-green blooms edged in maroon.

FINISHING TOUCHES

Once the shrubs, evergreen perennials, and bulbs (optional) have been planted, water the whole area thoroughly, and mulch with decorative chipped bark.

❊ **Pockets of bulbs** Plant dwarf, early-flowering daffodils like 'Tête-à-Tête' and Cyclamineus Group daffodils such as 'February Gold' to spring up between the bergenias and hellebores.

❊ **Sparkling backdrop** The simple combination of red stems and deep green foliage is enhanced by using a gold variegated shrub like *Elaeagnus pungens* 'Maculata' or *Elaeagnus* x *ebbingei* 'Limelight' as a foil.

❊ **Pruning for color** To achieve the intensity of stem color, plants like dogwoods (*Cornus*) must be cut back hard each year in early spring, before the new leaves expand (see pp.182–183), to encourage plenty of new growth.

MORE PLANT OPTIONS

HARDY BLOOMERS Winter heather (*Erica carnea* 'Springwood White' and *Erica* x *darleyensis*)

EVERGREEN GLOSS *Bergenia cordifolia* 'Purpurea'; *Bergenia purpurascens*; *Leucothoe* 'Scarletta'; *Pachysandra terminalis* 'Green Carpet'; *Skimmia japonica* 'Rubella'

GLOWING STEMS Color-stemmed dogwoods (*Cornus sanguinea* 'Midwinter Fire', 'Winter Beauty', and the yellow-stemmed *Cornus sericea* 'Flaviramea'); white-stemmed brambles (*Rubus cockburnianus*, *Rubus thibetanus*)

FLORAL SCULPTURE Christmas rose (*Helleborus niger*); Corsican hellebores (*Helleborus argutifolius*); stinking hellebores (*Helleborus foetidus* Wester Flisk Group); *Helleborus* x *hybridus* cultivars

Plants for shade

Designs for borders that don't get much direct sun tend to be quite muted with a predominance of white and pastel shades. This vibrant array of flowering and foliage plants features colors more often associated with hot, dry borders, but the ones chosen thrive on moisture-retentive soil and light or dappled shade.

🕐 GET THE LOOK

After incorporating bulky organic matter such as well-rotted, moisture-retentive manure or homemade compost into the soil (see pp.8–9), position the Japanese maple at the back. Set the clipped boxwood ball to the right of it, leaving a gap, and put the variegated hosta forward and to the left of the maple. Plant five orange *Geum* between the maple and the boxwood ball, and plant three *Heuchera* along the border edge.

FOLIAGE FLAIR
With their beautifully cut and often ruffled foliage, orange-leaf *Heuchera* and *Heucherella* varieties add a touch of leafy luxury to a partially shaded border.

AIRY HEIGHTS
Japanese maples like this *Acer palmatum* 'Sango-kaku' with its scarlet winter stems and delicate yellow-green leaves provide a tall focal point but cast minimal shade.

FLOWER FIZZ
Geum blooms are carried for weeks from early summer, as long as the soil is moisture-retentive and fertile. Dead-heading encourages repeat flowering.

FINISHING TOUCHES

Add a deep layer of well-rotted manure or homemade compost after thoroughly watering in the shrubs and perennials. This will help to retain moisture and counteract the rain shadow effect of the wall.

❋ **Dark contrast** Make the oranges and lime greens of this design sparkle all the more by contrasting with the bronze-leaf *Euphorbia amygdaloides* 'Purpurea' and the even darker foliage of *Actaea simplex* Atropurpurea Group.

❋ **Light reflection** To help the intricate shapes and textures stand out, provide a pale backdrop such as a treated wall or painted fence.

❋ **Fern fill** Use a range of shade-tolerant ferns to fill any holes you may have in the border. The copper shield fern, *Dryopteris erythrosora*, has colorful new growth and would work particularly well in this design.

MORE PLANT OPTIONS

FOLIAGE FLAIR *Acorus gramineus* 'Ogon'; *Carex oshimensis* 'Evergold'; *Heuchera* 'Key Lime Pie', 'Marmalade'; *Heucherella* 'Sweet Tea'

AIRY HEIGHTS *Acer palmatum* cultivars; *Calamagrostis brachytricha*; *Deschampsia cespitosa* 'Bronzeschleier'; *Molinia caerulea* subsp. *arundinacea* 'Transparent'

FLOWER FIZZ *Doronicum x excelsum* 'Harpur Crewe'; *Trollius* 'Golden Queen'; Welsh poppy (*Meconopsis cambrica*)

BOLD LEAF *Brunnera macrophylla* 'Jack Frost'; *Bergenia* cultivars; *Hosta* 'Sum and Substance'; *Rodgersia podophylla*

STYLISH CUT Golden yew (*Taxus baccata* Aurea Group); Japanese holly (*Ilex crenata*); variegated box (*Buxus sempervirens* 'Elegantissima')

BOLD LEAF

A single broad-bladed *Hosta* like the yellow variegated 'Frances Williams' will make a strong sculptural statement when surrounded by dainty blooms and fine-leaf foliage.

STYLISH CUT

Boxwood (*Buxus sempervirens*) is a useful shade plant, and when clipped into simple topiary forms like balls or cones (see pp.80–81) is a stylish feature.

Plants for poor soil

Ground made up of little more than rock shards is a boon for wild-garden enthusiasts. Nutrients rapidly wash out of the plant's rooting zone near the surface, making it harder for vigorous, weedy grasses to take hold and easier for wildflowers to establish. Rather than enriching your soil, just pick plants that like tough terrain.

GET THE LOOK

Divide a border with a wide gravel pathway. Plant three cotton lavender, two left, one right. Plant two bedding boxes (12 plants) of deep blue annual clary as a drift behind the two cotton lavender. Dot clusters of one, three, or five pot marigolds (*Calendula officinalis*), either side of the pathway, and plant a drift of heartsease (right). Sow annual field poppies in spring and fall in the gaps, or use Iceland poppy (*Papaver nudicaule*) plants for instant effect.

FOLIAGE COLOR
Annual clary (*Salvia horminum*) has flower bracts in purple-blue, pink, or white. Buy mixtures or single shades as seed or plants from the garden-center bedding section.

HILLSIDE SHRUBS
Cotton lavender (*Santolina chamaecyparissus*) is a drought-tolerant, evergreen, silver-leaf shrub, often grown in herb and Mediterranean-style gardens.

EASY ANNUALS
Hardy annuals like pot marigold (*Calendula officinalis*) can be sown directly in the ground, don't need rich soil, and self-seed generously into grit or gravel.

FINISHING TOUCHES

After watering plants, add extra touches to this dry garden design to create a wild hillside vibe. Then watch the bees and butterflies zoom in!

❈ **Gravel** On sandy soil without much visible stone, add gravel mulch to mirror the alpine hillside look and create a good self-seeding environment.

❈ **Rocks** Edge the pathway, and also create some stepping stones for maintenance access, sinking a few rounded boulders or flat-topped stones into the ground.

❈ **Ground cover** Use creeping alpines like stonecrops (*Sedum*), house leeks (*Sempervivum*), and creeping thymes to cover the ground around the rocks and stones.

❈ **Balance** Pull out annual grasses and other unwanted seedlings to keep a balance of bare gravel and to prevent dominant plants from crowding others out.

HERB GARDEN ESCAPEES

Heartsease or Johnny Jump Up (*Viola tricolor*) is a traditional herb garden annual or short-lived perennial that self-seeds well. It is a good plant for attracting bees.

PRETTY WEEDS

Field poppy or Shirley poppy, like other cornfield weeds, will only reappear when the ground is cultivated. Turn over the soil in its site each spring.

MORE PLANT OPTIONS

FOLIAGE COLOR Blue fescue (*Festuca glauca*); red orache (*Atriplex hortensis* var. *rubra*); sea kale (*Crambe maritima*); *Viola riviniana*

HILLSIDE SHRUBS *Cistus* x *hybridus*; creeping rosemary (*Rosmarinus officinalis* Prostratus Group); curry plant (*Helichrysum italicum*); lavender (*Lavandula angustifolia*)

EASY ANNUALS California poppy (*Eschscholzia californica*); love-in-a-mist (*Nigella*); poached egg plant (*Limnanthes douglasii*); sweet alyssum (*Lobularia maritima*)

HERB GARDEN ESCAPEES Borage (*Borago officinalis*); bronze fennel (*Foeniculum vulgare* 'Purpureum'); chives (*Allium schoenoprasum*)

PRETTY WEEDS Evening primrose (*Oenothera biennis*); fox and cubs (*Pilosella aurantiaca*)

Raised-bed gallery

Lifting planting above ground level has several advantages. It allows you to grow a wider range of plants if your soil is waterlogged, including those that require good drainage such as alpines and herbs. Aesthetically, raised beds also add interest to a flat site by creating different levels, and, set at the right height, you can minimize bending and even sit on the sides to garden.

◕ PRETTY AND EDIBLE

Raised beds are perfect for growing herbs since they have good drainage. This modern design has bold, repeating blocks of attractive vegetables, herbs, and edible blooms such as chives, ruby chard, bloody dock (*Rumex sanguineus* var. *sanguineus*), and oregano, with black-flowered violas as edging.

PLANT A HERB GARDEN
Add a drainage layer of debris to the base of the bed, and follow with gritty, loam-based compost or topsoil. Plant with contrasting clusters of flowers and herbs.

◕ CHUNKY TYRE PLANTER

In a contemporary setting, recycled tires, stacked to create planters, become edgy urban sculptures. Simply pile tires of the same diameter on top of one another, and line with a black plastic container or garbage can. Ensure the liner has drainage holes, and place a good depth of gravel or rocks (see pp.8–9) in the base before adding compost and planting.

BRIGHT IDEAS

There are many ways to construct and decorate raised beds. Pick a style that complements your garden's design. Raised beds made from sturdy wood planks, bricks, or treated wood with comfortable wooden or stone toppings can double as impromptu seating. As well as filling with plants, raised beds can also accommodate raised pools or sculptural features. Add LED recessed lighting to make the most of your raised structures at night.

WICKER COVERS

Put a stylish façade over cheaply constructed raised beds using woven wicker panels. To keep the wicker from rotting, paint with varnish, and raise off the ground on bricks or short legs.

STEPPED LUMBER

Here, in a new take on the traditional wooden-edged productive bed, a stepped bed of chunky railroad ties has been created with a strawberry bed, made with the same wood, set on top at right angles.

TABLE BED

You can nibble your way through this table decoration made up of edible flowers, salads, and herbs. The planter is recessed, giving the impression that the plants are literally growing out of the table.

Assembling a raised bed

For a quick and easy solution to a lack of planting space, try these stylish, wicker-sided raised beds. They come in a range of sizes and depths to suit different types of ornamental plants, herbs, and vegetable crops and can be ready for use in less than 30 minutes. They come complete with a liner bag with drainage holes and handles, which allow you to lift the basket if it needs moving after planting.

Here, flowering bedding plants have been used to add a splash of color to a graveled area, but you could also use compact-growing herbaceous perennials such as those listed opposite to create a long-lasting mini border. You can also put a number of wicker planters of different depths together to create a wide, tiered display on any hard surface—a paved driveway for instance.

1 Connect the wicker sides
Unfold the sides of the wicker planter, and stand them upright in the chosen location to form a rectangle. Use the small black plastic cable ties supplied with the planter to secure the corners.

2 Fit the liner bag
Open up the fabric liner bag that comes with the planter, and arrange it within the wicker walls. Plunge-water the plants (see pp.8–9), and set aside.

3 Fill the compartments
Holding the two compartments open with one hand, pour a little compost into each. This helps keep the liner sides upright. Continue to add compost, leaving space for the plants.

MORE PLANT OPTIONS

- ❋ **Agapanthus 'Peter Pan'**
- ❋ **Bloody cranesbill** (*Geranium sanguineum*)
- ❋ **Bugle** (*Ajuga reptans* 'Burgundy Glow')
- ❋ **Coral bells** (*Heuchera sanguinea* 'Snow Storm')
- ❋ **Daylily** (*Hemerocallis* 'Stella de Oro')
- ❋ *Diascia barberae* **'Ruby Field'**
- ❋ **Dwarf Shasta daisy** (*Leucanthemum* x *superbum* 'Snow Lady')
- ❋ **Heuchera** (colored foliage cultivars)
- ❋ **Penstemon 'Evelyn'**
- ❋ **Scabiosa columbaria 'Butterfly Blue'**
- ❋ **Modern pink** (*Dianthus* cultivars)
- ❋ **Red hot poker** (*Kniphofia* 'Little Maid')
- ❋ **Rhodanthemum 'African Eyes'**

4 Add the plants

Plant two *Impatiens* at the back and an *Osteospermum* between. Add a third *Impatien* in the center and a row of *Osteospermum* in front. Fill any gaps with variegated *Impatiens*. Water well.

Prairie planting

This natural-looking planting style of easy-care perennials and grasses works well in more rural locations where it can form a visual link to surrounding countryside. But it is surprisingly effective in contemporary settings too, where the billowing, diaphanous grasses and random flower swathes contrast with the crisp, clean lines of buildings, balconies, and paving.

GET THE LOOK

After thoroughly preparing the ground, lay out pre-watered pots, following the planting distance information on the plant labels. Start with a loose block of three of the same cultivar of *Helenium*, then arrange an arc of five to seven *achilleas* in complementary tones ranging from beige to deep tawny red. In between, plant a swathe of seven feather grasses dotted with three pots of *Allium sphaerocephalon*.

POP-UP DISPLAY
Summer-flowering bulbs like ornamental onions emerge from the ground, pushing up between the grasses to bloom, and then leave beautiful ornamental seedheads.

DAISY DAYS
Prairie daisies including *Helenium* are complemented by the linear quality and softness of grasses. Avoid having to stake taller varieties by pruning (see opposite).

BUTTERFLY BEACON
Colorful *Achillea* cultivars provide the perfect landing platform for butterflies that sip from the tiny blooms. Daisies and others from the list opposite also attract insects.

GRASSY HAZE
Be generous with *Stipa tenuissima*, weaving this gently self-seeding grass among the bold perennial flowers for a relaxed, natural effect.

FINISHING TOUCHES

After planting and thoroughly watering, continue to water during dry spells. This will ensure a more drought-resistant root system.

❋ **Do the "Chelsea chop"** Cut summer perennials back by about half in late spring to make them bushier, more floriferous, and self-supporting.

❋ **Get a late show** Leave flowerheads to mummify among the dry grass flowers.

MORE PLANT OPTIONS

POP-UP DISPLAY *Gladiolus communis* subsp. *byzantinus*; ornamental onion (*Allium hollandicum*); camas (*Camassia quamash*); Darwin hybrid tulips

DAISY DAYS Black-eyed Susan (*Rudbeckia fulgida*); Michaelmas daisy (*Aster* x *frikartii*); perennial sunflower (*Helianthus* 'Lemon Queen'); purple coneflower (*Echinacea purpurea*); *Coreopsis verticillata* 'Grandiflora' and *Coreopsis lanceolata*

BUTTERFLY BEACON Bee balm (*Monarda fistulosa*): *Asclepias tuberosa*; globe thistle (*Echinops ritro*); Joe Pye weed (*Eupatorium purpureum*); *Liatris spicata*; *Physostegia virginiana*; *Verbena bonariensis*

GRASSY HAZE *Miscanthus sinensis* 'Ferner Osten'; feather grass (*Pennisetum alopecuroides* 'Hameln'); feather reed grass (*Calamagrostis* x *acutiflora* 'Karl Foerster'); giant feather grass (*Stipa gigantea*); pheasant's tail grass (*Anemanthele lessoniana*); switch grass (*Panicum virgatum*)

English charm

The key to creating a English cottage-style garden is to adopt a relaxed, fluid approach to planting. Grow a jumble of ornamentals including delphiniums, marigolds, hollyhocks, geraniums, nasturtiums, and sweet peas, and mix with edibles including herbs, fruits, and decorative vegetables. Weave in softer-looking plants such as *Verbena bonariensis* and bronze fennel as a contrast to bold blooms like roses and Shasta daisies (*Leucanthemum*). Allowing some flowers to self-seed adds to the effect.

GET THE LOOK

For appeal, fill gaps in an existing border with some of the plants featured here. In a new bed, try an English rose at the back with three delphiniums in a loose cluster nearby. Add a French lavender and a medium-height Shasta daisy in front with a drift of 3-5 *Campanula* along the edge.

FRAGRANT ESSENCES
Aromatic herbs like lavender look and smell wonderful and have culinary and cosmetic value. Grow in well-drained soil in full sun, and clip lightly after flowering. For evening scents, try honeysuckle and *Hesperis matronalis*.

TALL STORY
Feathery-leaf fennel (*Foeniculum vulgare*) with its tall stems topped with flat golden flowers is attractive to hoverflies. It provides the perfect soft-focus backdrop to bold flower shapes like rose, dahlia, iris, and peony.

DAISY CHAINS
The childlike simplicity of daisies adds to the relaxed ambience of the English garden. Depending on how much room you have, choose between taller or more compact forms of the easily pleased Shasta daisy.

FINISHING TOUCHES

Rustic and reproduction elements add to the English look, as do recycled items. Surfaces should be muted, even distressed, to create a gentle backdrop.

❊ **Furniture** Go for assorted painted kitchen chairs around a stripped pine table or, for a less utilitarian look, find a wrought-iron set or perhaps a reproduction bench seat.

❊ **Groundwork** Gravel or slate chips are cheap and easy to lay, and desirable seedlings will pop up in gravel and soften large expanses. For more formality, edge borders with boards of pressure-treated wood, or lay brick pathways.

❊ **Containers** Put antique chimney pots and old kitchen pans into service as rustic flower pots, or use simple terra-cotta or lead-effect containers and wooden half-barrels.

❊ **Ornaments** English gardens offer a haven for wildlife, so a birdbath or beehive makes an ideal focus. Wicker and rusting wirework sculptures of wild and farmyard creatures also work well.

MORE PLANT OPTIONS

FRAGRANT ESSENCES Dame's violet (*Hesperis matronalis*); jasmine (*Jasminum officinale*); sweet pea (*Lathyrus odoratus*); sweet william (*Dianthus barbatus*)

TALL STORY Delphinium; foxglove (*Digitalis*); hollyhock (*Alcea rosea*); monkshood (*Aconitum*); mullein (*Verbascum*); penstemon

DAISY CHAINS Michaelmas daisy (*Aster*); pot marigold (*Calendula officinalis*), pyrethrum (*Tanacetum coccineum*)

BEE MAGNETS Cranesbill (*Geranium*); *Geum*; *Knautia*; *Verbena bonariensis*

ROSE ROMANCE *Rosa* 'Albertine' (rambler); *Rosa* 'Dublin Bay' (modern climber); *Rosa* 'Jayne Austin' (English)

BEE MAGNETS
With fruit and vegetables to pollinate, cottage gardeners used to include flowers like *Campanula persicifolia* to draw bees in. It grows in sun or shade and self-seeds lightly, forming drifts among the other plants.

ROSE ROMANCE
Perfumed shrub roses are important additions. Try English roses with their old-rose looks and good disease resistance. Provide well-manured soil or reasonably moisture-retentive soil, enriched with granular rose fertilizer.

Annual climber tripod

Annual flowering climbers arrive in garden centers in late spring, when they are sold alongside bedding and patio plants. When trained up a metal tripod or wigwam of poles, these plants can add height to your borders. Many annual climbers also have colorful, exotic blooms that lend a subtropical atmosphere.

You can grow lots of these climbers yourself from seed if you sow them in pots on a warm window ledge in early spring. If you don't have time to do this, you can buy plants that have already been hardened off or acclimatized to outdoor temperatures.

You will get the best results from your plants if you position them in a sunny, sheltered spot so that they are out of the path of any turbulence and wind.

1 Prepare the pot
Put a layer of drainage material in the base of the pot. Cover with compost so the top of the root ball is about an inch below the rim after planting.

2 Plant the three climbers
Mix a little slow-release fertilizer into the rest of the compost. Place the three climbers in the pot, and add the compost around them. Firm lightly and water well.

3 Replace the supports
Evenly space three stakes around the pot. Cut away the ties holding the climbers to their support stakes, remove them, and loosely tie the stems to the new stakes.

For a rustic English-garden look, grow plants up a support made from decorative twisted twigs and raffia (as shown here) rather than the more mundane bamboo poles secured with wire plant ties or twine. A mulch of rounded pebbles placed on top of the soil continues the English-garden theme.

Sweet peas or climbing nasturtiums (see panel, right) also have the requisite old-fashioned charm and don't need a hot summer to perform well.

MORE PLANT OPTIONS

* **Black-eyed Susan** (*Thunbergia alata* 'African Sunset')
* **Canary creeper** (*Tropaeolum peregrinum*)
* **Chilean glory flower** (*Eccremocarpus scaber*)
* **Cup and saucer vine** (*Cobaea scandens*)
* **Morning glory** (*Ipomoea purpurea*)
* **Nasturtium** (*Tropaeolum majus*, climbing variety)
* **Spanish flag** (*Ipomoea lobata*)
* **Sweet pea** (*Lathyrus odoratus*)
* **Twining snapdragon** (*Lophospermum scandens*)

4 Complete the tripod

Using a piece of raffia, tie the tops of the stakes securely, and finish with a double knot. Use short lengths of raffia to hold the stems of the climbers in position.

5 Trim the stakes

Neaten the top with shears, cutting the stakes to the same length. Add the mulch. Train overlong stems back down the tripod for an even spread of blooms.

Urban chic

Though some of the planting in this outdoor room is reminiscent of traditional English-style gardens, the gridlike framework and sleek, hard-landscaping features give it a contemporary look. A restrained color scheme of grays, purples, and whites creates a tranquil feel, perfect for an urban retreat. Graceful grasses add height without stealing space, and easy-care flowers keep maintenance low.

DESIGNER GRASS
The airy specimen grass used here is giant feather grass (*Stipa gigantea*). It has an evergreen base and "see-through" flower stems that last into the fall.

🕐 GET THE LOOK

In a rectangular border extending out from the house wall, plant one giant feather grass (*Stipa gigantea*) at the far end. Plant a clipped boxwood cube behind it on one side and another diagonally opposite, further back. In the compartment created by the staggered boxwood and grass, plant three or five French lavender (*Lavandula pedunculata* subsp. *pedunculata*). Fill the remaining space close to the wall with a white-flowered hydrangea.

GREEN ARCHITECTURE
Boxwood (*Buxus sempervirens*) topiary provides year-round interest, acts as a crisp foil for flowers, and, shaped into topiary blocks, echoes the form of buildings.

PURPLE HAZE
The French lavender (*Lavandula pedunculata* subsp. *pedunculata*) is slightly tender but otherwise low maintenance. It is drought tolerant and produces many tufted blooms.

COOL WHITES
Hydrangea Endless Summer® 'The Bride' adds a sophisticated note with its apple-green-then-white blooms. Dig in organic matter before planting.

FINISHING TOUCHES

Pink climbing and patio roses, fresh white marguerite daisies, and purple dwarf veronicas complete the look. Plant remaining beds and walls over time using wall shrubs, climbers, and single specimens, surrounded by blocks or drifts of flowers such as nepeta and verbascum (pictured).

* **Shades of gray** Blue-gray door and window frames and darker weatherboarding give a contemporary backdrop.
* **Pebble panels** For added texture, push small pebbles into mortar, and tamp down with a wooden straight edge.
* **Boxed beds** Walk-around beds allow for easy access and bring fragrant and aromatic plants right into the sitting and dining space.
* **Crisp lines** A rigid grid pattern of beds and paving works well for this modern courtyard.

MORE PLANT OPTIONS

DESIGNER GRASS *Calamagrostis* x *acutiflora* 'Overdam'; *Miscanthus sinensis* 'Gracillimus', 'Kleine Fontäne', 'Morning Light'; *Pennisetum alopecuroides* 'Hameln'; *Stipa calamagrostis*

GREEN ARCHITECTURE Bay (*Laurus nobilis*); holly (*Ilex aquifolium* 'J.C. van Tol'); Japanese holly (*Ilex crenata*), *Pittosporum tenuifolium*; yew (*Taxus baccata*)

PURPLE HAZE *Allium hollandicum* 'Purple Sensation'; *Lavandula* x *intermedia* 'Grosso'; *Nepeta* 'Six Hills Giant'; *Salvia* x *sylvestris*; *Solanum crispum* 'Glasnevin'; *Verbena bonariensis*

COOL WHITES *Choisya* x *dewitteana* 'Aztec Pearl'; *Hydrangea paniculata* cultivars; *Magnolia grandiflora* 'Exmouth'; *Trachelospermum jasminoides*; *Viburnum plicatum* 'Mariesii'

Smart features

Your garden can be a great place to explore your creative side with simple topiary, DIY sculpture, and other garden arts. Using imaginative landscaping techniques, you can easily add some designer flair, and you may also be surprised at how readily you can transform existing elements into eye-catching features or new wildlife habitats. Many practical elements, such as lighting, can also be decorative.

Outdoor lighting

Installing outdoor lights creates opportunities for enjoying views of the garden at night, whether inside or out. Low level and recessed units keep glare to a minimum while making walkways safe, but some lights are used more for decorative effect and are easy to add.

STRINGS OF LIGHTS

LED strings for outdoor use are available in various lengths. Simple white "fairy lights" are easily accommodated, but there's a wide range of styles and colors. Plug the cords into an outlet inside a garage or shed with power. Use a solar-powered set to dress up a potted topiary (see below).

TRELLIS SPARKLE
Allowing sufficient length to plug in to an undercover power strip, wind string lights around posts and through screens.

PERGOLA DECOR
Use colorful and novelty string lights to brighten up a plain foliage backdrop or liven up a bare pergola.

BRIGHT IDEAS

A wealth of lighting systems is available from home improvement stores, including safe low-voltage types that run off outlets with extension cords. Simply mix and match a variety of light fittings. Use solar post lights to light up a pathway or border and solar lights strands around shrubs or trees. For larger projects, with lights running directly off the electrical system, you must consult a qualified electrician.

MOBILE LIGHTS (FAR LEFT)

Lanterns and colored-glass tea-light holders look good day or night. Hang from shepherd's hooks, and use to complement the colors in your borders.

PARTY TIME (LEFT)

Bright paper lanterns create a party atmosphere on a still summer's evening. Hang at different heights from a pergola or an overhanging branch.

LIGHTING THE WAY (ABOVE)

Set tea lights in glasses half-filled with sand along pathways, and at the edges of patios and decks. The sand stabilizes the candle and absorbs its heat. Terra-cotta pots with chunky low candles also work well.

ROOM AT NIGHT (LEFT)

This secluded terrace is lit for both aesthetic and practical purposes, but the light levels are low and arranged to avoid glare, giving the space a restful feel. LED uplighters graze the walls with a gentle glow, illuminating foliage and creating soft shadows. Changes in level are lit for safety, but candles and lanterns are arranged purely to enhance ambience. Never leave naked flames unattended.

Shapely topiary

YOU WILL NEED
Topiary shears (A small pair of two-handed conventional shears or a battery-operated trimmer is also suitable.)
Piece of strong wire (e.g. galvanized fencing wire)
Pliers
Sprayer containing rubbing alcohol for sterilizing cutting blades
Hand brush

Although you might feel that you don't have the skills or the time required to train more complex topiary shapes such as this ball-headed spiral form, the good news is that you can buy pieces that are ready-grown. Plant them in large pots to decorate the patio, or set them into a border creating an eye-catching focal point.

But how to keep such works of art looking as good as the day you purchased them? Provided you don't allow the topiary to get too shaggy and overgrown, giving it a "haircut" is a relatively quick and easy job. Trim boxwood plants between late spring and the end of the summer to avoid frost damage.

If you don't have any topiary shears, a small pair of two-handed conventional shears or a rechargeable, battery-operated trimmer can be used instead.

1 Trim the base
Starting at the base, begin to cut back the new growth, following the original shape of the coils as closely as possible. Lift small potted topiary onto a raised surface to avoid bending down.

2 Shape the head
Trim the ball-shaped head by eye initially. Walking around the topiary as you work allows for more accurate shaping and makes clipping less tiring. Cut out any dead parts.

3 Check progress
Make a simple frame by bending a piece of fencing wire into a circle and twisting the two ends together with pliers. Moving it around the head, use it to help you shape the sphere.

TIMELY ADVICE

* **Remove dead matter** Shake dead leaves from topiary interior, and remove clippings because they may harbor fungal disease.

* **Water regularly** Boxwood needs good drainage and cool, moist roots. Water pots routinely, even after rain. Red-tinged foliage is due to stress from excess heat and dryness.

* **Avoid granular feed** Boxwood is surface rooting, and granular fertilizer is too concentrated; it damages the roots and causes foliage scorch. Liquid feed or mulch with well-rotted manure instead.

* **Air and light** Occasionally turn potted topiary if it is positioned against walls and hedges. This promotes even growth and prevents sections from dying due to a lack of light. Good air circulation curbs diseases.

4 Sterilize tools
To lessen the risk of transferring diseases like box blight from one piece to another, sterilize shears in between plants by spraying the blades with rubbing alcohol. Also, dispose of any plant debris.

Instant ivy topiary

If you like adding a touch of stylish formality to your garden in the form of topiary but don't feel confident clipping classic evergreens like boxwood or yew, ivy-covered wire frames are a great substitute. You don't need special skills, and if you start with plants with long trails, the results are virtually instant.

Ready-made frames have legs that you insert into pots or directly into the ground.

Traditional shapes are cones, spheres, and ball-headed standards, but some companies make a huge range of styles that include birds and other animals.

For neatness, use plants with single-color leaves and short joints (the distance between leaf and stem). For frames without wire, just wind the ivy up and across the struts. The leaves will act like grappling hooks, holding the stems in position.

1 Plant the ivy
Plunge the ivies into a bucket of water to soak. Put a layer of drainage material in the pot, add the compost, then plant the ivies equally spaced.

2 Add the frame
Remove bamboo canes and any ties from the ivy. Separate the stems and lay them out as shown. Push the legs of the frame into the compost.

3 Arrange the ivy
Starting at the bottom of the frame, wind each ivy stem in an upward spiral. Attach the stems to the wire mesh with ties, or tuck in the shoot tips.

TIMELY ADVICE

❋ **Add follow-up feed** The slow-release fertilizer stops working after about six months, so water with a nitrogen-rich liquid fertilizer to maintain healthy growth.

❋ **Fingertip prune** Snipping off the soft shoot tips of the ivy promotes side-branching and ensures that the frame becomes densely covered.

❋ **Be on pest alert** In spring and early summer, guard against aphids on the new growth by rubbing them off or blasting them with a jet of water.

❋ **Clip topiary** Once the frame is fully covered, use small hand shears or scissors to trim the ivy. If the plants become thin and woody-stemmed with age, cut them away, and replant the frame.

4 Water to grow

Water well, and place temporarily in a sheltered, lightly shaded spot to speed growth. Keep tying in new growth until the frame is covered. Trim off any excess.

Streamlining shrubs

If you find yourself running out of planting space, consider removing or drastically pruning some of your existing shrubs. Left to their own devices, most evergreens will sprawl to cover a lot of ground, excluding light and preventing anything from growing underneath. But if you raise the height of the lowest branches and superimpose a more formal shape on the rest of the shrub, you can turn a shapeless blob into a stylish feature plant or small tree. What is more, the newly revealed branches can be remarkably sculptural.

If you like, you can replenish the soil beneath your streamlined shrub so that you can underplant with a colorful display of ground cover, herbaceous perennials, or shrubs. Or, as in the case of this bay, use the space for a seating area or pot grouping.

1 Assess the shrub
This overgrown bay has two distinct sections—a large domed head, the base of which needs raising slightly, and a proliferation of shorter branches around the base. Try to visualise the final shape.

2 Remove larger branches
Hold back the foliage to assess the internal structure. Wearing gloves, remove some of the bulk with loppers, then finish with a pruning saw. Make a saw cut beneath branches first to avoid splitting.

3 Neaten the cuts
Trim thicker branches so that they are almost flush, avoiding unsightly stumps, and remove twiggy growth with shears. Your aim is for the crown to be supported by several shapely, sinuous stems.

SUITABLE PLANTS

* **Bay** (*Laurus nobilis*)
* **Boxwood** (*Buxus sempervirens*)
* **Escallonia** cultivars
* **Holly** (*Ilex aquifolium* and *Ilex x altaclerensis* types)
* **Laurel** (*Prunus laurocerasus, Prunus lusitanica*)
* **Laurustinus** (*Viburnum tinus*)
* *Magnolia grandiflora*
* *Osmanthus x burkwoodii*
* *Pittosporum tenuifolium*
* **Privet** (*Ligustrum ovalifolium*)
* **Rhododendron** (taller, large-leaf types)
* **Silk tassel bush** (*Garrya elliptica*)
* **Yew** (*Taxus baccata*)

4 Finishing touches

Further reduce the crown and shape with shears or pruners to produce a more even or formal dome. Rake up debris. Weed, then mulch or improve the soil by adding garden compost or well-rotted manure.

Decorating walls and fences

The vertical surfaces of house walls and boundaries offer tremendous scope for enhancing the garden. From simple paint and stain treatments to a little visual trickery, most of the ideas explored here are straightforward but can have a big impact on the look and feel of a space.

◐ MIRRORS

Reflective surfaces make outdoor spaces feel larger. Use glass mirrors, sealed to prevent the silvering from peeling off; plain or colored plastic mirror panels; or sheets of stainless steel. Large mirrors capturing a perfect reflection of greenery are dangerous to birds, so overlay with trellis and plants, or place statues in the foreground.

DOUBLE THE IMPACT
Use clips to fix an old mirror to a wall, and then hook a flower-filled half-basket to the front.

◐ CREATING ILLUSIONS

To trick the eye into thinking the garden goes beyond its boundaries, try fixing a salvaged door and frame to a plain wall or fence. Grow evergreen wall shrubs and climbers around it, and flank with a matching pair of planters. A shuttered window with mirror back or arched mirror with matching trellis façade and foreground sculptural element will also open up the confines of a courtyard.

TROMPE L'OEIL
Attach a false-perspective trellis-and-mirror set to a wall, and place a bench in the foreground to create this trick of the eye.

◐ FEATURE WALLS

Treat a section of brick or painted wall to a glamorous makeover using tinted masonry paint available from home improvement stores or paint stores. First, clean off grime and algae, then work over with a wire brush to remove loose material, and seal with diluted PVA glue. Select a bold color for extra drama, and accessorize using planters. A second neutral shade like white can be used for remaining surfaces.

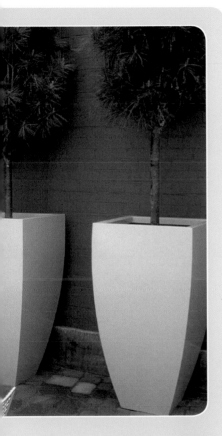

BRIGHT IDEAS WITH PAINT

Exterior paints and stains transform walls and fences fairly cheaply. If you want a particular color, it can usually be mixed for you. Use contrasting shades to highlight features such as raised beds or alcoves. Express yourself with simple stencils, or use color to set the mood for outdoor dining.

EDGE EFFECT
For a contemporary touch or to revive faded lumber, apply a bold paint-stain product to wooden-sided raised beds.

ABSTRACT STYLE
Transform a dreary outlook with some abstract curves. Outline the shapes first, and then fill them in with a small brush.

HOT HOUSE
Set the scene for a collection of tropical-looking patio plants using an orange or lacquer-red painted backdrop.

BRIGHT IDEAS WITH ADD-ONS

There's a wide range of decorative metalwork panels available from garden stores, but you can make your own wall ornament too. Water features are usually complete packages ready to plug in.

WALL FOUNTAIN
Position a mask above a barrel or pebble-topped hidden reservoir with pump. Camouflage wires and tubing with plants.

PLANTERS
Buy or make a wooden rack. Attach it to a wall with sturdy screws and wall plugs, and use it to suspend planters.

ON SHOW
This simple but stylish primrose theater, used to showcase potted *Primula auricula* specimens, provides shade for the plants.

COLORED PANELS
Make your own wall art with vibrant color squares on a pale backdrop. Outline shapes with broad masking tape before painting.

Inspired planters

YOU WILL NEED

Soft pencil or chalk

Fabric wall planter with pockets

Hammer and galvanized masonry nails

Trowel

Multi-purpose potting compost

Sufficient plants to fill one per pocket (*Petunia* Cascadias Bicolor Purple shown here)

Bucket of water for plunging plants

These handy fabric planters can be fixed up in no time, and, planted with colorful bedding, they will create instant impact on a bare wall. Unlike hanging baskets, they don't stick out very far, and this makes them useful for decorating narrow spaces such as side passages or small courtyards.

As an alternative to flowers, you could also fill these planters with different varieties of cut-and-come-again salad leaves; herbs like basil, parsley, coriander, and oregano; or even cascading 'Tumbler' tomatoes.

In fall, consider cramming the pockets with single displays or mixtures of small hardy spring bulbs like crocus, *Anemone blanda*, *Scilla sibirica*, or the dwarf daffodil 'Tête-à-Tête'. Alternatively, you can empty them, dry them thoroughly, then fold them away for the winter.

1 Fix to the wall
Mark a level on the wall to act as a guide for fixing. Nail one corner, stretch the planter taut, then nail the other corner. Add a couple of nails between for extra holding power; a full planter will be heavy.

2 Fill the pockets
Partially fill each of the pockets with moist potting compost, allowing sufficient room to accommodate the root balls of your chosen plants, in this case, petunias.

3 Begin planting
Prepare the plants for planting by plunging them in a bucket of water first. Wait until the bubbles stop, indicating the root ball is saturated. Plant and add some more compost.

MORE PLANT OPTIONS

❋ **Sun-loving plants** *Sutera* Copia Series, *Sutera cordata* 'Snowflake', *Bidens ferulifolia*, *Lysimachia congestiflora* 'Outback Sunset', million bells (*Calibrachoa*), *Nemesia* cultivars, *Scaevola aemula* 'Blue Wonder', Swan river daisy (*Brachyscome multifida*), trailing geranium (*Pelargonium*), trailing snapdragon (*Antirrhinum*), *Diascia* hybrids, *verbena* (trailing cultivars)

❋ **Shade-loving plants** *Begonia sutherlandii*, *Impatiens*, fuchsia (compact trailing varieties), violas and pansies, wishbone flower (*Torenia*), *Begonia* (fibrous-rooted varieties), *Impatiens* New Guinea hybrid, Monkey flower (*Mimulus × hybridus*), *Solenostemon scutellaroides*, Variegated mints (*Mentha* cultivars), *Primula* Wanda hybrids

4 Firm plants in, then water

Firm the soil lightly with your fingers. Ensure there is a gap between the soil surface and rim of the pocket to allow water to pool before soaking in. Water thoroughly, pouring slowly.

Special occasions

Whether celebrating a special date or simply wanting to create a magical look for a dinner party, there are a number of simple yet stylish ways to dress the table and make the gathering memorable. Most decorations can be prepared in advance, leaving more time to organize the food and drink. Cut fresh flowers in the cool of morning or evening, and leave to soak out of direct sunlight in a cool room until needed.

LIGHT EFFECTS
At dusk flickering candles add a romantic touch. Here, glass and metal-handled tea-light holders are hooked on a branch to light the table.

 **GET THE LOOK**

String up the tea lights and bunting from a secure stepladder, and then move the trestle table and chairs into position underneath. Lay a cloth and table runner followed by the place settings, each plate topped with a rolled napkin secured with a napkin ring and a tiny sprig of leaves and blooms. Set out glasses, tea-light holders, and a couple of mini bouquets, and place a large jug of flowers at one end.

FABRIC DECOR
Bunting adds a festive note. Make your own color-coordinated version. This bunting is made from triangles of inexpensive fabric remnants attached to string with craft glue.

FLORAL FOCUS
A simple ceramic pitcher filled with wildflower lookalike blooms in white and soft blue adds a fresh, country-garden touch to the table.

MINI BOUQUETS
Colored drink glasses make good substitutes for vases. Fill with identical arrangements of flowers and foliage picked fresh from the garden.

FINISHING TOUCHES

If you have time, there are lots of extra touches and flourishes you can add to delight your guests and enrich the outdoor-dining experience.

❈ **Color theme** Here all the "ingredients" are drawn from the same narrow palette of colors, creating a fresh, springlike feel.

❈ **Chair backs** Use colored ribbon to attach a hand-tied bunch of aromatic herbs such as lavender and rosemary to each chair back.

❈ **Napkin sprigs** Tuck a few pieces of greenery into each napkin ring, or bind the stems with florist's wire or tape, and make a tiny nosegay for each setting.

❈ **Table runner** The fresh white runner with green leaf motif makes a lovely visual contrast with the darker cloth. Long, trailing stems of ivy also make a good foliage runner down the center of the table.

MORE DECORATIVE OPTIONS

LIGHT EFFECTS Add a Gothic touch with candelabras wound with ivy. Lay wilt-resistant evergreen foliage down the center of the table, intertwined with battery-operated twinkling lights. Hide the small battery pack under leaves.

FABRIC DECOR If dining beneath a pergola, hang billowing lengths of colored voile or muslin (see pp.34–35) to match your color scheme. Use the same material to make oversized chairback bows.

FLORAL FOCUS Try topping each place setting with a water-filled bowl containing floating rose petals or whole blooms.

MINI BOUQUETS Surround a single rose with frothy flowers like lady's mantle (*Alchemilla mollis*), or just have a few stems of variegated foliage instead.

Pebble beach

Adding a sweep of stones and pebbles is a fun and simple way to enliven a plain graveled area of the garden. They introduce textural contrast and, when wet, gleam and show off their subtle colors and markings. To create a natural-looking beach or stream bank effect, use stones of at least two different sizes, but stick to similar shades. The addition of the turquoise glass or acrylic chips or beads—available from garden centers and craft stores— helps to suggest a rock pool on a sunny beach.

You can lay the pebbles in a broad, sinuous band around a deck, but this project also works particularly well in corners or within circles where you can form crescent shapes.

If you have a shady area, consider running a swathe of gravel through a planting design of hostas and ferns.

1 Position the stones
Place the large rock in the gravel, positioning it off-center. Place larger stones around it to form a loose curving band. Add smaller stones and pebbles in random clusters in front and behind.

2 Add the colored beads
Scatter opaque beads in a gap between rocks, using them more densely in some areas. Layer over some transparent beads to create the illusion of a pool of water.

3 Position the grass
After plunge-watering (see pp.8–9), plant the grass in its pot, leaving a gap below the rim for a gravel mulch and to allow for watering (see pp.8–9). Water and place among the pebbles.

BRIGHT IDEAS

Add more plants to strengthen your beach or seaside theme. Blue and silver-leaf grasses and alpines, drought-tolerant perennials, and succulents work well. Theatrical props are fun too.

SUCCULENTS AND SHELLS

A tender agave looks good set among a collection of scallop shells (available at fish markets), pebbles, and gravel.

ROPE COILS

The color of old, weathered rope coiled into a circle is the perfect beachcomber element to subtly suggest the coast.

AHOY THERE!

Some props shout "beach." Try a life ring or fisherman's net, or use an anchor to complete your look.

Placing sculpture

In order to discover the best site for a newly acquired piece of sculpture, experiment with different settings. If it is heavy or awkward to maneuver, substitute with a pile of boxes or even a plastic garbage can.

◔ PLACING SMALL PIECES

It can be tricky to know how to position a small ornament in a garden because it can seem lost and out of scale with its surroundings. Try mounting it on a wall or pergola post, placing it in an alcove, or setting it on a spotlit platform.

IN THE POT
Animal sculptures look good peeping out from beneath plant foliage in a border or at the foot of a potted plant.

FLOOR DETAIL
If placing the animal beside the pot, link the two together by scattering the pot's slate mulch beside the sculpture too.

◑ GROUNDING

Arrange sculptural elements so that they are properly integrated with the garden. One way to do this is by anchoring the piece with planting so that it appears to be rising out of the ground. Rather than putting a sculpture in the middle of a lawn, create more intrigue by setting it half-hidden in the border or at a pond's margin.

BRIGHT IDEAS

You can make much more of decorative elements, even simple pieces, by positioning them to draw the eye. Utilize the contrasting color and texture of any backdrop to your advantage, and perhaps pair up or group objects for greater emphasis. Consider the footprint of the garden, the layout of patios, pathways, lawns, borders, and pools, and site sculptural elements at key points.

DRAWING THE EYE
The geometric layout creates intersecting sight lines—the perfect spot for this classical vase. Let perspective guide the eye to objects at the end of pathways, lawns, or pools.

REPETITION
Placed at regular intervals, this row of topiary standards, set against a plain, colored backdrop, makes a dramatic statement. You can use metal or painted wooden obelisks in a similar manner.

USING DRIFTWOOD
The weathered look of driftwood gives an informal feel to an area. Try upright pieces among see-through grasses, or group to create interest in a border. Alternatively, lay horizontally among pebbles and gravel.

TOPIARY
Clipped shrubs add weight to a border of airy flowers. Use these green architectural elements to create paired sentinels at an entrance or to emphasize a change in direction or level.

LIGHT AND AIRY
More delicate or intricately-shaped pieces of sculpture should have a plain backdrop to allow you to appreciate their form in detail. A plain wall, clipped hedge, lawn, or gravel expanse is ideal.

COLLECTOR'S CORNER
Whatever it is that you enjoy collecting, group the pieces artfully to focus attention on them. Small items will look best arranged around a larger object—this will help to hold them together visually.

Mini waterlily pond

YOU WILL NEED

Shallow ceramic planter without drainage holes or a container plus plugs to block any holes

---

3 fine-mesh aquatic planting baskets and plastic netting (optional)

White pygmy waterlily (*Nymphaea tetragona*), small reed mace (*Typha minima*), American blue flag (*Iris versicolor*)

Aquatic compost and washed pea gravel

You can create your own tiny oasis on a sunny patio by planting a miniature pond with a choice selection of petite plants. Don't be surprised if dragonflies come to investigate!

Center stage is the white pygmy waterlily, whose rounded leaves float on the surface, cutting down the amount of light reaching the water, which keeps algae at bay. The diminutive reed mace and iris create vertical contrast. Here, this simple ensemble takes on an Asian flavor with a backdrop of woven willow and pebbles.

To avoid limescale, use soft water to fill the planter or, better still, rainwater, which is chlorine-free. Gravel in the pots keeps the compost in place underwater.

1 Prepare a planting basket

Add aquatic compost to the bottom of a mesh planting basket. Unless the mesh is fine, lay a square of plastic netting in the bottom first to retain the compost.

2 Plant the waterlily

Set the pygmy waterlily in the basket, leaving enough space on top of the soil for the gravel topping. Fill in around the sides with more aquatic compost.

3 Add the gravel topping

Cover the compost with gravel, then water gently to settle the compost around the roots without disturbing it. Repeat Steps 2 and 3 for all the plants.

4 Fill the planter

Add water to the planter, leaving sufficient room to accommodate the volume that will be displaced by the planting baskets when they are in position.

5 Submerge the basket

Gradually lower the baskets into the water. If planting into a deeper container such as a half-barrel, you may need a brick to support the pots at the correct depth.

MORE PLANT OPTIONS

❋ *Acorus gramineus* 'Ogon'
❋ **Corkscrew rush** (*Juncus effusus* f. *spiralis*)
❋ *Houttuynia cordata* 'Chameleon'
❋ *Iris versicolor* 'Kermesina'
❋ **Water pennywort** (*Hydrocotyle umbellata*)
❋ **Miniature horsetail** (*Equisetum scirpoides*)
❋ *Nymphaea* **'Pygmaea Helvola'**
❋ **Parrot's feather** (*Myriophyllum aquaticum*)
❋ **Water lettuce** (*Pistia stratiotes*)
❋ **Umbrella plant** (*Cyperus* species, especially dwarf forms)
❋ **Water hyacinth** (*Eichhornia crassipes*)
❋ *Eleocharis acicularis*
❋ *Lysimachia nummularia* **'Aurea'**

DIY sculpture

You don't have to spend money to acquire sculpture, as the ideas here show. Discover what pleases you, and don't be afraid to try some more unusual projects. The garden makes an ideal gallery in which to work; try using man-made objects, such as rusting ironwork, as well as natural materials.

◉ STONE SPIRALS

This shape frequently crops up in the natural world and works on a small or large scale. Arrange white pebbles on fine gravel, or, for extra drama, use shiny black pebbles on white gravel. Alternatively, overlap smooth slate chips.

◉ TERRA-COTTA MOBILE

Made from hand-thrown clay pots and string, this quirky hanging can take on a variety of looks and could include colored beads for more color. Suspend from a hanger as shown, or tie from a branch or pergola.

LINK TOGETHER
String up pots, the top one upright, the others upside-down. Use pieces of hose or wood to secure the knots.

PLANT TOP POT
Fill the upright pot with compost, and plant a drought-tolerant hens and chicks (*Sempervivum*).

BRIGHT IDEAS: CLEVER ARRANGING

Many ordinary objects can be transformed into sculptural elements simply by arranging them in a defined pattern—a circle of flat stones buried end-up in the ground, for example. When using natural materials, your artwork can be transient and experimental. Some sculptures will rot or blow away over time, but that's part of their charm. You can suspend or wall-mount them for a different look.

BRIGHT IDEAS: WILLOW WORKS

Grow your own supply of coppiced willow if you have room (cut back hard each winter for a fresh crop of unbranched "wands"), or buy online, although soak these on arrival to restore their flexibility. Alternatively, most deciduous garden shrubs have pliable stems, so use ones accumulated from pruning.

WILLOW ARCHWAY

Push a row of long stems deep into the ground on either side of the path. To complete the overhead section, attach more stems using string. Finally, plant more wands, and weave in at an angle.

ECO ART

Look for logs with attractive or intriguing bark colors and patterns; gnarled pieces are especially sculptural. Bury partially in the ground, and vary the height and girth along the line.

DRIFTWOOD STACK

Use a cordless drill to drive a hole through the middle of assorted pieces of bleached driftwood. Thread with heavy-duty galvanized wire, and rotate pieces to complete the sculpture.

GREEN LINE

Save drinks bottles from the recycling bin, and turn them into contemporary artwork. Dig a narrow trench into which you can insert them, upturned. Pale gravel shows off the color well.

LEAFY BOWER

If you want willow to sprout, plant when dormant. Make the basic framework and door opening first with lashed poles. Plant other willow wands, and weave into the framework at an angle for strength.

ORGANIC FORMS

These larger-than-life willow balls can be bought online. They have an intriguing textural quality, and the simple egg shapes or flower pods look right at home on the edge of a wildflower meadow.

Light up a shady corner

Shade cast by buildings and mature trees is a common problem with today's small plots, but by using shade-loving plants, perhaps grown in raised beds or planters to avoid root competition from trees, as well as pale and reflective surfaces and decorative elements, you can create your own tranquil oasis.

MIRRORED SURFACES

Install a polished stainless-steel water feature nestled among ferns to add a magical feel to your shady spot. Safe, low-voltage fountains like this come with a hidden reservoir and submersible pump included, and run off a power strip.

PALE PLANTERS

Plant white planters to add light to areas without borders. This boxwood's shape is echoed by the stones beside it.

ANTIQUE ELEGANCE

Create a pleasing tableau in a dull corner with just a couple of props. Here, the intricate detail of a cast-iron table is thrown into relief against dark bamboo. A single chair would also work. Add period detail with an old-fashioned watering can, and in the sunlit foreground, try planting a white rose and a white agapanthus.

BRIGHT IDEAS

The contemporary garden (left) shows how variegated plants such as hostas and ivies, yellow *Miscanthus* grass, and glossy-leaf plants such as *Fatsia japonica* and x *Fatshedera lizei* can reflect the light.

MODERN MINIMALISM

This shade garden is lifted by treating the plain wooden fence and bench with a simple but effective pale-gray wood stain.

ZEN SIMPLICITY

Take inspiration from Japanese gardens and use pale gray boulders, stones, and gravel to create restful landscapes. The white wall highlights the maple's delicate foliage.

ROOM OUTSIDE

A soft furnishing palette of cream through to pale apricot adds light to this tiny courtyard and ties in well with the sandstone paving. White stones act as a focal point, anchored by lush planters.

GHOSTLY TREES

The startling white bark of the birch *Betula utilis* var. *jacquemontii* adds sparkle to a gloomy patch of garden. Here, the multi-stemmed trees rise out of shade-loving ferns and astilbe.

Lawn into meadow

If you have a lot of regularly mown grass in your garden, you might want to consider converting some of it in order to create a wild meadow effect. If you don't routinely use selective lawn weedkillers, you might be surprised at the number of wildflowers that you find growing in the turf. Stop mowing, and let the grass grow to see these wildflowers bloom. Introduce some other wildflowers for extra effect.

GET THE LOOK

Mark out the areas you want to convert into meadow, using posts and string as guidelines. The shapes can either be organic with meandering pathways or formal, perhaps a sequence of squares or rectangles. Starting in the spring, begin mowing regularly, but leave the marked areas to grow. After skipping a few cuts, you will be able to see the areas clearly against the short lawn, and then you can remove the string.

BEE FAVORITES
Red clover (*Trifolium pratense*) bears its nectar rich blooms all summer, providing an important food stop for bees, butterflies, and other insects.

TOUGH WHITES
The ribwort plantain (*Plantago lanceolata*) is a survivor even on dry ground, producing abundant brown poker heads, each with a haze of tiny white blooms. Its deeply veined leaves are narrow and pointed.

YELLOW HAZE
Floating over the top of long grass, the cup-shaped blooms of meadow buttercup (*Ranunculus acris*) produce an eye-catching display. It is ideal for slightly damp or heavy ground.

DAISY DAYS
The ox-eye daisy (*Leucanthemum vulgare*) can be easily introduced to your converted lawn as a plug plant (see "Add plants" opposite). The iconic blooms produce a instant meadow look.

FINISHING TOUCHES

At first your meadow might contain mostly grasses, but even these add a wild feel when in flower. Follow the advice below to enhance the look.

❋ **Maintain pathways** Keep a crisp edge between long and short grass. Make main thoroughfares wide, and cut regularly.

❋ **Add plants** To speed up colonization, buy plug plants from specialty wildflower nurseries, and plant in fall or spring into short turf. Naturalize bulbs.

❋ **Weed** Dig out coarse weeds, such as dock, bramble, tree seedlings, and rapidly colonizing weeds such as thistle and dandelion, or spot-treat with glyphosate weedkiller.

❋ **Cut and clear** At the end of summer, cut your meadow with a string trimmer. Leave material for a few days to allow seed to drop, then remove hay with a rake. This keeps coarse grasses from reproducing and encourages self-seeding.

MORE PLANT OPTIONS

BEE FAVORITES *Stachys officinalis*; field scabiosa (*Knautia arvensis*); *Centaurea nigra*; mallow (*Malva sylvestris*); meadow cranesbill (*Geranium pratense*); selfheal (*Prunella vulgaris*); speedwell (*Veronica chamaedrys*); tufted vetch (*Vicia cracca*)

TOUGH WHITES Cow parsley (*Anthriscus sylvestris*); white clover (*Trifolium repens*); wild carrot (*Daucus carota*); yarrow (*Achillea millefolium*)

YELLOW HAZE Bird's foot trefoil (*Lotus corniculatus*); cowslip (*Primula veris*); *Galium verum*; St. John's wort (*Hypericum perforatum*); yellow rattle (*Rhinanthus minor*)

DAISY DAYS Common cat's ear (*Hypochaeris radicata*); daisy (*Bellis perennis*); fox and cubs (*Pilosella aurantiaca*); hawkbit (*Leontodon*)

Shaping a lawn

YOU WILL NEED

Measuring tape

Bamboo pole and string

Sand or can of white, line marker spray paint

Half-moon turf cutter

Sharp border spade

Lawn edging strip

Fine slate chips, decorative gravel, or fine milled decorative bark

Superimposing a sharply outlined shape onto an ill-defined lawn area transforms the look of the whole area. Geometric forms give a sharp, contemporary look, but a simple circle fits any style. Don't worry if the space you have won't accommodate a whole circle. A simple arc with rectangular shapes cutting in to it looks just as good.

For larger lawns, play around with different combinations—two overlapping circles, for example. The trick to getting the look is to cut a precision edge.

Lawn edging strip is essential if you are mulching borders with a stone aggregate, but cutting a vertical edge, pulling back the border soil, and mulching with bark also works.

1 Measure up
Decide on the new shape for your lawn, and sketch it out on paper. To create a curve, first measure out a square with a tape measure, marking the corners.

2 Mark the circumference
Place a bamboo pole at the corner of the square opposite where your curved edge will be. Attach a string to it, then pulling the string taut, marking out the edge of the circle with sand.

3 Cut out the shape
Use a half-moon tool or a flat spade to cut a vertical edge, following the sand line. This separates the turf cleanly, and the slot will be used later for the edging.

4 Remove the turf
On newly laid turf, grass should peel back, but on established turf, use a sharp border spade to slice through the roots, removing a generous depth of sod.

5 Add the lawn edging
Push lawn edging strip down into the slit you made previously. The edging should be fractionally below the lawn surface, allowing you to mow over it easily.

6 Fill with slate
To define the shape and hide the edging, add fine slate chips or gravel. To protect mower blades from damage, the mulch should be just below the strip.

Stepping stone path

YOU WILL NEED
Paving slabs
Old sharp kitchen knife or utility knife
Small sharp spade
Soft sand
Bag of ready-mixed mortar (optional)
Bucket and trowel
Ramming tool or short plank of lumber
Rubber mallet

Paths are needed for all-weather access in the garden, but they can sometimes be very obtrusive, especially if your garden is small. If that's the case, consider stepping stones. Here, they are laid into a lawn, but they are also useful set through deep borders so that you can reach plants easily. On a firm base, such as a well-used lawn, you probably won't need mortar to stabilize the slabs, although sand is useful for leveling.

Stepping stones make a lovely feature leading to a garden seat or a bird bath, but the route must be practical—too many detours and people will take shortcuts over the grass.

1 Position the slabs

Experiment with laying out the slabs. Walk your proposed path to ensure that the steps you take are comfortable. Cut around the first slab to mark its position, then put it to one side.

2 Cut away the turf

On newly laid turf the grass will readily peel back, but on established grass you'll need to cut through the roots with a small, sharp spade. Keep the spade virtually level with the ground.

3 Remove the soil

Dig out enough soil to accommodate the slab, allowing it to sit just below the lawn surface—this will make mowing easier. If you are using mortar, remove an extra 2–3in (5–8cm).

4 Add the sand

Pour sand into the bottom of the hole, and compact it with a ramming tool or piece of wood. In most cases this will make a sufficiently firm base for the slab.

5 Add the mortar

If the ground is soft or you want to ensure the slab doesn't slip, add some ready-mixed mortar combined with just a little water. Spread the dryish mix out evenly with a trowel.

6 Set the stone in

Place the slab into the hole and, if using mortar, gently tap into position with a rubber mallet. If you're only using sand, you may need to remove or add some in places to prevent it from rocking.

Grow it, eat it

Any garden, no matter how small, can be a productive garden. You can utilize most surfaces, including walls and windowsills, for growing crops. Whether you grow fruits, vegetables, herbs, and salads on their own or mix them together with flowers, your productive displays can also be highly decorative. Most crops can be grown in containers, and many provide tasty treats in a matter of a few short weeks.

Trained fruit

Training stems of fruit trees in neat arrangements on fences and walls is an elegant and space-saving way of growing your own. It makes use of bare vertical spaces while allowing underplanting too.

PERFECT PLANTS

Walls and fences laden with juicy, brightly colored, ripening fruit are a mouthwatering sight in summer. Training fruit trees takes a little work initially, but once established they will provide you with a bountiful harvest without too much maintenance. Tie in new shoots as they grow, and prune away unwanted ones, and you will have productive and decorative plants that can be used as features or divisions within a garden.

⏱ SUPPORTS

Young shoots need tying in to train them in the right direction, but more mature branches also need support when laden with fruit. There is a variety of supports you can use for this job, depending on the surface you are training against and the effect you want to create.

WIRES

If you have a wooden fence, affix strong horizontal wires at 15in- (35cm-) intervals between the posts, securing them to rings.

FIGURE-EIGHT TIE

When tying stems to stakes, use a figure eight. The string then sets between the stake and the stem, which prevents rubbing.

BAMBOO FAN

First fix horizontal wires to a fence. Tie two bamboo poles in the middle to create a cross shape, and push the cane ends into the ground in front of a vertical support. The main branches need to be tied in to the vertical support as well as the horizontal and angled ones to create a fan shape.

SINGLE CORDON (LEFT)

You can produce a high yield from just one upright or angled stem. This is ideal in small plots. Try apples, pears, white currants, red currants (pictured), or even gooseberries.

APPLE ESPALIER (ABOVE)

This perfectly proportioned tree can be grown as a dividing fence or against a wall. Train the main stems horizontally to create a balanced, even framework.

BLACKBERRIES ON WIRE (ABOVE)

Training blackberries doesn't have to involve complicated shapes; just tying in sprawling stems to a framework of horizontal wires makes maintenance and harvesting easier.

APPLE STEPOVER (LEFT)

The ultimate space-saver, these low-growing, horizontally-trained trees make perfect edging plants along paths or borders, or to divide beds. Despite their diminutive size, they produce surprising amounts of fruit.

PEAR DOUBLE CORDONS

These U-shaped trees look sharp when grown in a row and create an attractive and productive boundary. This technique is suitable for apples and pears that produce fruit on spur-bearing sideshoots. Support plants with wires or against walls.

Blueberry pot

PLANT Mid-spring to fall
HARVEST Summer to early fall

YOU WILL NEED

Large decorative pot, bigger than the plant's original pot

Compost for acid-loving plants for the container

Trowel or compost scoop

1 potted blueberry plant (*Vaccinium*) in a pot (2- or 3-year-old potted plants will establish more quickly than bare-root ones)

The blueberry is a great dual-purpose plant, earning its place on the patio for its juicy, superhealthy berries as well as its pretty, ornamental appearance. In the summer abundant crops of delicious berries follow clusters of dainty white flowers, and once the crop has been harvested in the fall, the plant treats you to a dramatic display of leaves in a range of reds and purples.

Blueberry plants are ideal for container growing, especially if you have neutral or alkaline soil, since they require acid soils. This is easily achieved in pots by using acid-based compost.

Although some blueberry varieties are self-pollinating, others require a partner to bear fruit. However, if you have space, buy a second variety because they fruit more prolifically if they have a companion plant.

1 Prepare for planting
Place some drainage material on the base of the pot. Cover the crocks with a layer of acid-based compost—enough to cover, but leave space for the plastic pot.

2 Position the pot
Remove the plant from its plastic pot, and place the pot centrally inside the larger container. Backfill around the container with more acid-based compost.

3 Firm in
When the level of the compost is about 1in (2.5cm) below the rim of the larger pot, press down on the compost to firm it in place but not compact it.

TIMELY ADVICE

❊ **Favorite drink** Water the plant in well when first planted, and then continue to water at regular intervals during the growing season, particularly in hot weather. If possible, use rainwater to avoid raising the soil's pH level.

❊ **Seasonal treat** Each spring, apply an annual top dressing of acid-based compost along with half the recommended rate of acid-based fertilizer.

❊ **Mulch down** Apply a 3in (7.5cm) layer of acid-based mulch, such as leaf mold, on top of the soil each spring. Pine needles or conifer clippings are also good.

❊ **Room to grow** Compact varieties are best for pots, but even these may need more room. If the plant looks cramped, pot in the spring into a larger container.

4 Plant up

Carefully remove the plastic pot without disturbing the compost "sides." Tease out the plant's roots, lower it in, and plant at the level it was in the original pot.

Container fruit

Whether you have a large garden or a small patio, putting fruit in containers is a practical and attractive way to grow your own. With a little care and attention, the plants will thrive and reward you with an abundant crop of delicious, homegrown fruit.

⏱ CARING FOR YOUR PLANTS

Fruit grown in containers requires a little more care than those in the ground because they are reliant on you to provide the food and water they need to survive and flourish.

FEEDING
Feed fruit trees every spring using a balanced fertilizer. Prepare the fertilizer according to the instructions on the packet.

NETTING
Protect your fruit crops as they grow by covering them in mesh netting, but make sure birds can't get trapped under it.

⏱ REPEAT POTS

Individual pots placed strategically on a patio or deck make a statement, but if you have room, repeating matching pots planted with the same fruit draws the eye. The arrangement is also good for plants that are not self-pollinating—they need to be planted in groups.

PERFECT SOIL
Planting in containers enables you to grow fruit that may not be suited to your garden soil. Plants such as blueberries, blackberries, and cranberries need acidic soils, which can be provided in any garden with a pot of acid-based compost.

PERFECT PLANTS

Many plants have specific growing requirements, and most gardens couldn't accommodate all of them, so by growing in pots you can provide the perfect conditions for each and every plant. Containers naturally restrict the growth of fruit trees, which means you can be sure that the plants will remain the right size for your space without needing a lot of pruning.

SPACE-SAVING TREES

Fruit trees such as apples, pears, cherries, plums, damsons, and apricots are all available on dwarf rootstocks, which are suitable for growing in pots. This restricts their growth and improves their vigor, and in turn their productivity.

FROST-TENDER PLANTS

Container-growing means you can include tropical or frost-tender plants, such as oranges or lemons, in your garden. Plant them in lightweight pots, and move them indoors when the nights turn chilly and frost threatens.

Strawberry basket

PLANT Early to mid-spring
HARVEST Early to late summer

YOU WILL NEED

14–16in (35–40cm) lined basket

Large pot for support

Multi-purpose potting compost with added soil-based compost

Scissors

Slow-release fertilizer granules

Water-retaining gel crystals (optional)

3–5 strawberry plants (choose a mixture of varieties for a long season of fruiting)

Strawberries make attractive hanging basket plants and are ideal if you don't have much growing space. This method of cultivation means you don't get fungal damage from soil splash, and it stops slugs and snails from eating the fruits.

Plant a mixture of varieties with different cropping times to ensure a long season of fruiting. In return for regular watering and feeding, you should be able to pick a few strawberries every few days for a couple of months.

When planting in strawberry beds, it's best to remove the first season's flowers to encourage a strong root system, but that isn't the case with baskets. Planting in the spring with pot-grown plants allows you to crop in the first year and, if you're are a little late planting, you can use garden-center plants that have already started to flower.

1 Prepare the basket
Set the basket on top of a large pot to steady it. Cut a few drainage holes in the lining, a third of the way up the sides. Leave the bottom intact to retain water.

2 Add the fertilizer
Ensure plants don't run short of nutrients by adding slow-release fertilizer to the compost. You can also add water-retaining gel crystals.

3 Plant the basket
Plunge the strawberry plants in a bucket of water, then space them evenly in the basket. Plant them at the same depth as they were in their pots. Gently firm the compost around the plants.

TIMELY ADVICE

❋ **Water regularly** Plants can rot in soggy compost, so don't overwater, and keep water off of foliage to avoid fungal diseases.

❋ **Fertilize** Use liquid tomato fertilizer once flowers begin to form.

❋ **Ensure even light** Turn the basket weekly to ensure that the fruits ripen evenly.

❋ **Remove runners** New plants form at the end of stems; remove to improve fruiting. Freshly cut runners can be rooted in lightly shaded pots of moist compost to create new stock. In strawberry beds, root runners in the soil before severing.

❋ **Encourage a second year of fruiting** Take the basket down at the end of the season, and remove old leaves. The following spring, replenish the compost with fertilizer.

4 Leave to acclimate

After watering, stand the basket in a sheltered spot to get over the shock of planting. Leave for around 10 days, then hang the basket on a sunny wall.

Edible climbers

If you're short of space on the ground, growing climbing fruit and vegetable plants is an excellent way to make use of vertical spaces and maximize your cropping potential. Fences and walls in sunny spots are ideal locations, but plants will also happily climb posts, pergolas, trellis, and obelisks in beds and borders.

◔ CLIMBING STRUCTURES

Make a feature out of your practical plants by growing them up and over decorative supports. The plants will quickly scramble and cover posts and frames, adding height to a design and raising the fruit and flowers into the sunlight and the pathway of pollinating insects.

BAMBOO
Wigwams and tripods of bamboo poles provide a traditional framework for beans and peas.

PERGOLA POST
Wires attached to posts provide support for climbing plants and make it easy to tie in stems.

ARCHED WALKWAYS
Arches add a decorative element to a garden and look great with fruit and vegetables hanging down from above. Lash together pliable prunings with twine for a rustic look.

PERFECT PLANTS

Wherever there's a sunny wall or fence in your garden, there's an opportunity to grow your own food. Nail wood strips to fence posts or walls, and attach wires or trellis panels to these. These will provide support for your plants as well as ensuring there is good air circulation around them.

CUCUMBERS

These climbing plants need help to grow up supports and benefit from stems being secured at intervals to trellis or frames.

VERTICAL GRAPEVINE

A hot and sunny wall is the perfect place for a vine. With regular pruning and initial tying in, the plant will scramble up supporting wires and reward you with a delicious harvest of sun-warmed grapes.

TOMATOES

Bush and cordon (single-stemmed) tomato plants can be trained up bamboo stakes. Tie in the stems as they grow, and to encourage fruiting, pinch off the sideshoots that grow between the leaf joints and main stem.

SQUASH

Squash need lots of room, so growing them in bamboo and rope nets raised above the ground frees up ground space and lifts fruits away from hungry slugs.

Growing herbs

Herbs make wonderful ornamental features in window boxes, in borders, or in their own self-contained space. In addition to being pretty, herbs have been valued for their medicinal and culinary properties for hundreds of years. Nothing beats the flavor of freshly picked herbs in favorite recipes or teas, or the fragrance of the leaves as you brush past them on a summer day.

🕐 GET THE LOOK

This classic circular herb garden contains a useful mixture of annual and perennial herbs. To achieve a similar look, plant a fennel and three pots of chives in a 1ft- (31cm-) diameter pot in the center of a prepared 3ft- (1m-) diameter circular bed located in a sunny, sheltered spot. Divide the ground below into five wedges. In each one, plant three pots of each herb: parsley, thyme, marjoram, mint, and variegated sage.

TASTY TEXTURES
Moss-curled parsley is a biennial herb best grown as an annual from seed in late spring. The delicate, frilly leaves hide a big appetite; they need deep, compost-enriched soil.

MAGIC CARPET
Thymus 'Silver Posie' is a pretty, evergreen thyme that bears pale pink flowers in summer above silver, variegated leaves. Cut with shears after flowering to keep it compact.

MEDITERRANEAN FLAVOR
Unlike pot marjoram (Origanum vulgare), sweet marjoram (Origanum majorana) is best grown as an annual to get the most out of its aromatic, pale green leaves.

FINISHING TOUCHES

Water your herbs regularly, more so in dry conditions. If herbs shoot up in hot weather, nip off the growing tip; this will encourage the plant to bush out.

❋ **Radiating lines** Line the edges of each segment with stones. Clip plants after flowering to keep them compact so they don't encroach into other wedges or outside the circle.

❋ **Groundwork** To emphasize the shape of your herb garden, surround it with bricks laid in a radiating pattern. Alternatively, dig a shallow trench around the perimeter, and lay bricks diagonally on their side against each other.

❋ **Ward off weeds** When annual herbs die off in winter, cover the bare soil with waterproof membrane, and scatter over some gravel. It is a more attractive look and keeps weeds away until you are ready to sow again in spring.

❋ **Central theme** If your central plant becomes too big or overpowers the design, replace it. A small standard bay in a pot would suit this spot.

MORE PLANT OPTIONS

TASTY TEXTURES Coriander (*Coriandrum sativum*), chervil (*Anthriscus cerefolium*), lovage (*Levisticum officinale*)

MAGIC CARPET Chamomile (*Chamaemelum nobile* 'Treneague'), creeping thyme (*Thymus serpyllum* var. *albus* or *T. serpyllum* 'Snowdrift'), *Rosmarinus officinalis* Prostratus Group

MEDITERRANEAN FLAVOR Basil (*Ocimum basilicum*), rosemary (*Rosmarinus officinalis* 'Sissinghurst Blue'), silver sage (*Salvia argentea*)

SCENTED WONDERS Pineapple sage (*Salvia elegans* 'Scarlet Pineapple'), orange-scented thyme (*Thymus* 'Fragrantissimus'), lavender (*Lavandula angustifolia* 'Hidcote')

VIBRANT COLORS Basil 'Purple Ruffles', lemon balm (*Melissa officinalis* 'Aurea')

SCENTED WONDERS
The purple-tinged leaves of the mint *Mentha* x *piperita* f. *citrata* have an eau-de-cologne scent. It grows vigorously in well-drained soil enriched with well-rotted manure.

VIBRANT COLORS
The dramatic, variegated evergreen foliage of *Salvia officinalis* 'Tricolor' makes up for its mild flavor. To ensure a good supply of leaves, prune after flowering.

Spicy leaves

Don't stick to the same leaves for your salad bowl; the joy of growing your own means you can try something different. There is a good selection of spicy leaves available now that will add zing and zest to your salad. These are generally sold as seed mixes, such as Italian, Asian, or spicy leaf selections. Choose the variety that best suits your palate and style of cooking.

GET THE LOOK

Sow seeds in pots filled with multi-purpose compost with added soil-based compost. Follow the instructions on the packet for the appropriate planting depth and distances according to the variety you choose. Read the packets carefully when buying—spicy mixes can be very spicy, so make sure you choose one with your preferred level of heat! Water seeds in well, and thin out seedlings as they appear, watering and weeding around them regularly.

CUT-AND-COME-AGAIN
You can keep salads tasty all summer long with cut-and-come-again varieties. Mizuna has a light mustardy flavor and is ideal for shady patios; it dislikes extreme heat.

COLORFUL CROPS
Hot spicy salads look great with unusual, colorful leaves in them. Exotic varieties such as 'Red Komatsuna' are easy and speedy to grow, even in cooler climates.

EXTENDED HARVEST
Some leaves can be sown in early spring in warm ground or under cover and will crop into the fall. Frilly-leaf, Greek cress leaves are happy under cloches into winter.

FINISHING TOUCHES

A container full of colorful spicy leaves can brighten up a patio or garden in summer as well as liven up your salads. Keep them happy for a long harvest.

❊ **Fill the gaps** Cut-and-come-again seeds are best for providing a harvest for the whole season without needing to resow, but if there are gaps, sow seeds into them to bring on new plants.

❊ **Gravel mulch** As the seedlings appear, scatter some fine gravel over the surface of the compost to keep down competing weeds and to conserve moisture in the summer months. Many greens will bolt if their soil conditions become too dry.

❊ **Mix and match** Pots look great grouped, so plant a number of containers with a variety of salad mixes; perhaps an Italian blend in one, Asian in another, textured leaves in another.

❊ **Winter warmers** As the plants near the end of their harvesting life, sow seeds of one of the many winter varieties that are available for a year-round crop.

OTHER PLANT OPTIONS

CUT-AND-COME-AGAIN Corn salad; mizuna; purslane; endive

COLOURFUL CROPS Radicchio; ruby chard; red giant mustard; golden purslane; kale 'Red Russian'

EXTENDED HARVEST Buckler-leaf sorrel; land cress; winter purslane; Texsel greens; endive 'CanCan'

A TASTE OF ASIA Bok choy 'Golden Yellow' or 'Canton White'; Chinese cabbage 'Golden Yellow'; Chinese mustard; tatso; mustard 'Red Frills'

SALAD SEASONING Watercress, parsley, mustard 'Green Wave', Italian dandelion 'Red Rib'

A TASTE OF ASIA
It's hardly surprising that many spicy leaves have Eastern origins. Crops such as red mustard are favorites in Asian cooking and are often sold in stir-fry seed mixes.

SALAD SEASONING
Let the salads season themselves; you won't need to add pepper if you include leaves that have their own spice. Arugula is an invaluable salad ingredient with a peppery kick.

Kitchen-door salad

PLANT Mid-spring to early fall
HARVEST Late spring to early winter

YOU WILL NEED

Broad container with holes for drainage

Layer of drainage material (see pp.8—9)

Loam-based potting compost

General-purpose fertilizer granules

Purchased salad plants or salad strips
(e.g. chard, spinach, beets, cut-and-come-
again or loose-leaf lettuce, Asian greens,
radicchio or herbs)

A mix of tasty salad leaves right by the kitchen door means that you can pick a meal no matter the weather. Many salads can be harvested a few leaves at a time, which allows the plant to put out more shoots and replenish your supply. Here, we've used rainbow chard, but any purchased salad plants will do. Alternatively, sow seeds of quick and easy crops like cut-and-come-again lettuce.

You can plant up any broad, waterproof container as long as it has drainage holes; colored vinyl tubs work well if you drill some holes in the base.

If you are using a metal container, line it with cardboard to protect the plant roots from excessive heat. To reduce moisture loss from terra-cotta pots, line with compost bags with holes cut in for drainage.

1 Fill the container

Put a layer of drainage material in the container. Fill almost to the top with a loam-based potting mix or with a 50/50 mixture of general-purpose compost and topsoil.

2 Prepare to plant

Work in a general-purpose granular fertilizer following the packet instructions. Pre-soak the pots or strips of vegetables. Gently remove the salad plants, separating individual plants at the roots.

3 Plant and press in

Scoop out a planting hole so that the plant will be at the same planting depth as it was in its original container. Insert the plant, backfill with potting compost, and lightly firm around the plant base.

TIMELY ADVICE

❋ **Keep a full watering can handy** Leafy crops need lots of moisture, so water early morning and, if very hot, in the evenings too. After the initial watering, get the water straight to the roots by watering at the base of the plants.

❋ **Feed well in summer** Even after adding granular fertilizer, your salad will run out of steam after a few months. Feed with a liquid fertilizer for leafy crops.

❋ **Protect from pests** Watch out for slugs and snails when it's wet and in the evenings. Take a light out at night to catch them. Push in thorny twigs to deter cats.

❋ **Keep warm** Drape fabric over the pot during cooler weather to prolong harvesting.

4 Find a bright spot

Continue planting, allowing about 2½in (6cm) between each plant. Water well, then stand the container in a well-lit location. Plant a group of containers to give a variety of leaves.

Winter salad

When summer is over, you don't have to head back to the supermarket for your salad; you can grow winter salad leaves just as you would summer varieties. There are a great many hardy or specialized winter varieties available, and if planted in well-drained soil and picked regularly, they provide a continuous crop until spring.

FABRIC

Hardy varieties of salad leaves will survive cold weather, but if the temperatures are forecast to plunge well below freezing and frost is forecast, give plants a helping hand by providing them with some warmth. Horticultural fabric will prevent frost from damaging susceptible seedlings and plants while still letting through essential light and rainwater.

PLANT BOX
Plant young plants such as these chard 'Bright Lights' in a box of multi-purpose compost.

ADD HOOPS
Push bamboo hoops into the soil, and cover with fabric, making sure it does not rest on the leaves.

CLOCHE

A cloche acts like a mini greenhouse, keeping the soil warm and the frost off plants. They are traditionally shaped like a bell and so are best used for individual plants. However, tunnel cloches are available if you want to protect rows of plants. Cloches block airflow, so they must be removed to ventilate plants on warm days.

USING A CLOCHE
Select the plant you want to protect, and place the cloche over it without damaging the leaves.

ROWS OF PLANTS
If you need to protect several plants, cover each with its own individual bell cloche.

PERFECT PLANTS

Many hardy summer salad varieties will happily provide you with leaves year-round, but there is also a wide range of varieties available that have been bred specifically for winter use. They tend to have a stronger, more robust flavor, and some are a little bitter. If you wish, blanching leaves by covering them with an upturned flower pot will reduce the bitterness.

RADICCHIO
Despite its Mediterranean origins, this Italian leaf chicory is hardy, and its flavor becomes sweeter as the weather gets colder. Its red, mottled leaves provide a welcome splash of color in the winter.

WINTER PURSLANE
Claytonia perfoliata, known as winter purslane or miner's lettuce, produces small, rosette-shaped plants from early winter to late spring. The fleshy, succulent leaves can be eaten in salad or steamed like spinach.

MIZUNA
These peppery, serrated salad leaves are not unlike arugula in flavor and appearance. They can be grown year-round but are perfect winter crops since they dislike hot weather and prefer cool, wet conditions.

TEXEL GREENS
Also known as Ethiopian greens, these fast-growing salad leaves are related to cabbage but have a flavor that is similar to spinach. They are ideal for growing as cut-and-come-again crops all year round.

Funky pots

Don't feel that you have to stick with a certain style or look when it comes to containers—your garden can reflect your own personality and tastes, so have some fun! You can use pretty much anything you like to grow your own, just add drainage holes. So dig out those funky containers!

JUICE CARTONS

Don't confine fruit juice cartons to the recyling bin; give them a new lease on life in your garden first. Cut off the tops, pierce some holes in the bottom, fill with compost, and plant with annual herbs.

CUT THE BOXES TO THE SAME HEIGHT
The boxes you use don't have to match, but the arrangement does look better if they are all trimmed to the same height.

MILK CARTONS

Plastic milk cartons may not be the most attractive container, but when overflowing with salad leaves and carefully positioned as a group, they create a quirky-looking living wall.

TIE UP WITH STRING
Pierce a hole in the side of each bottle near the rim, and tie some string through it. Attach the other end to a drainpipe or nails in the wall.

BRIGHT IDEAS

Some plants just cry out for a colorful container—brightening up the garden on an unseasonably dark day. Have fun with containers of all colors, shapes, and sizes. You can recycle practically anything, including worn-out footwear, used packaging, or spare kitchen equipment.

COLANDER

You won't need drainage holes in this pot, but it does need lining with a waterproof membrane to prevent soil loss. The shiny material glinting in the sun may even keep birds off the precious fruit!

RAIN BOOTS

These bright red boots are the ideal height to double as a strawberry planter. Plant on top, and cut holes in the sides for more plants. Rain boots also work well for root crops such as carrots or parsnips.

BUCKET OF TOMATOES

Don't throw out a battered bucket. Make some drainage holes, hang it, or nail it to the wall, and let tomatoes tumble down.

BAGS OF VEGETABLES

These bags are a funky take on a growing bag and will add color and style to your patio. Perfect for a zucchini plant, or try putting three seed potatoes in each one.

PACKING CRATE

Wooden packing crates can be a stylish feature. Line the sides with old plastic compost bags to prevent rot and prolong the crate's life, then plant it with climbing squash, figs, or kiwi.

Sprouting seeds

Even those without a garden can enjoy the satisfaction of growing their own produce, such as sprouting seeds. These delicious, nutritious shoots can be grown from seed in just a matter of days, any time of year—perfect for the impatient gardener or as an activity with children.

Specialty sprouting containers are available online or from health-food stores, but it is just as easy to use a clean glass jar with a perforated lid. There is a good selection of seeds available from garden centers or online suppliers, so choose those you like to eat best. Once big enough, the sprouts can be steamed and used in salads, sandwiches, and stir-fry dishes.

For a continuous crop of sprouts, start a new jar of seeds sprouting every couple of days; then you will always have some ready when you need them.

1 Soaking seeds
Place the seeds in a jar, and put on the perforated lid. Add enough water to cover the seeds, then set the jar aside in a warm place out of direct sunlight overnight.

2 Rinse off
The next morning, drain away the water through the perforated lid. Rinse the seeds in fresh water in the jar twice daily, draining it away again each time.

3 Harvest time
Continue to rinse and drain the seeds every day. They are ready to eat when the sprouts have reached 1in (2.5cm) long. Rinse the seedlings well before use.

TIMELY ADVICE

❋ **Clean and fresh** Make sure that the jar you use for sprouting seeds is thoroughly washed in hot soapy water before use.

❋ **Let them breathe** The seeds need air to germinate, and poor air circulation will cause them to rot. If your jar doesn't have drainage holes, cover it with fine muslin instead, and secure with an elastic band. Do not use a sealed, airtight container.

❋ **Rinse regularly** Rinse seeds every 12 hours to prevent mold from developing and to help remove seed hulls.

❋ **Cook carefully** Current guidelines recommend that you should not eat these shoots raw for health reasons. Steaming until hot is the best way to cook them to preserve their nutrients and vitamins.

Vegetables from seed

PLANT Mid-spring to fall

YOU WILL NEED

Short bamboo stakes and string

Length of lumber and a dibber or trowel

Seeds (carrots shown here)

Enough horticultural fabric to cover the seedbed

You can buy many vegetables as young plants, ready grown, but it is far more economical to grow them from seed if you have the space. Some varieties can be sown directly into seedbeds or vegetable beds, soil conditions and weather permitting, while others are best started off under cover and planted out when the temperatures have warmed up.

Always prepare the ground well before sowing. It needs to be turned over and fed with well-rotted manure well in advance, and then raked to a fine tilth when you are ready to sow. This makes it easier for the delicate roots of the seedlings to find their way through the soil.

Planting in drills makes thinning and weeding much simpler because you can clearly identify the leaves of your crops and run less risk of hoeing up developing seedlings.

1 Preparing to sow

Mark out the drills using lengths of string tied between stakes. Using the edge of a piece of wood and a dibber or trowel, make the drill in the prepared soil.

2 Sow seeds

Sprinkle the seeds evenly along the length of the drill, following the instructions on the seed packet. Gently cover with soil without displacing them.

3 Protect seedlings

Water seedlings well in dry weather. If frost is forecast, cover the developing seedlings with a layer of fabric, and lightly pin it down at the sides. Fabric is also good for protecting crops from flying pests.

TIMELY ADVICE

❄ **Sowing seeds indoors** Sow seeds into individual pots, modules, or seed trays filled with potting compost.

❄ **Keep warm** Put sown seeds in a cool greenhouse or on a windowsill indoors until they have germinated.

❄ **Harden off** After the last frost, prepare seedlings for outdoor living by gradually exposing them to temperatures outside.

4 Thin out

Gently pull out seedlings along the row until they are at the recommended growing distances. Compost thinnings away from the beds—in particular carrots to prevent attracting carrot flies.

Container crops

Most fruit and vegetables are ideal candidates for container-growing. You don't need a vegetable garden or a rented plot to grow your own; use your space creatively, and you can place pots around the garden to make use of sunny, sheltered spots. Walls, steps, windowsills, and patios all are good homes for healthy plants and need only a little planning.

PLANTING A WINDOW BOX

The kitchen window ledge is ideal for a box of homegrown salads or herbs since it is easy to reach out and pick them as needed. Sow cut-and-come-again varieties for a constant crop.

COPPER STRIP
Attach a copper strip around the sides of the container. This will give slugs and snails a shock and stop them from devouring your harvest.

PLANTING IN GROWING BAGS

These are handy for growing tomatoes, zucchini, or squash in smaller gardens. Throw away the bags at the end of the growing season, and dig the compost into borders.

CUT A HOLE
Knead the bag to fluff up the compacted compost inside. Lay it flat, and cut a hole in the plastic around a cardboard collar.

PLANT UP
Make a hole in the compost, then remove each plant from its pot. Put a plant in each hole, and backfill with compost. Firm in.

WATER AND FEED
Water plants in growing bags well, and feed regularly as fruits form; the compost will quickly become depleted in nutrients.

BRIGHT IDEAS

Colorful crops lift a garden in summer, and if you are intermingling your containers with ornamental plants in beds, borders, or patios, why not choose fruit or vegetables that will provide a splash of color as well as a tasty harvest? You don't have to stop there—use containers that are interesting or brightly colored to show off your homegrown produce to best effect.

WINDOWSILL CROPS

Chili peppers provide a welcome blast of heat in the summer, and the dramatic red fruits will warm up any windowsill.

PLANTING POCKETS

Living walls are a beautiful, textural feature, and these clever planting pockets will provide a prolific herb harvest.

COLORFUL TRUGS

English trugs are one of the most versatile pieces of garden equipment, and work well as containers. With drainage holes, one large trug can hold two rhubarb plants, giving a good harvest from a small space.

RADIANT RADISHES

Juicy radishes are quick and easy to grow, and if planted successionally, you can enjoy the crunchy texture of these cheery red roots from late spring until early fall, plucked from a pot right by your back door.

TIN BATH

Line metal pots with compost bags to stop the compost from drying out too quickly.

STEPPED PLANTERS

These stylish willow boxes hide the plastic liners beneath and make a smart feature along the top of a wall or lining wide steps.

PAINTED POTS

The joy of ceramic and tin pots is that you can paint them any color to match your mood, to reflect your personal style, or to contrast or echo the colors of the fruit or vegetables planted in them. All they need is a coat of outdoor paint, and they have a whole new lease of life.

Sack of potatoes

PLANT Late winter to mid-spring
HARVEST Early to mid-fall

YOU WILL NEED

Tubers (seed potatoes) grown from virus-free stock (select based on cropping time, resistance to disease, cooking use, color, and texture).

Egg carton

Black trash bag and burlap bag or other large container

Loam-based potting compost

Scissors or shears

Potatoes are one of the easiest crops to grow in containers. You can use any large recycled pots and tubs as long as they have drainage holes. For a rustic look, use a lined burlap bag, shown here, rolling up the sides as you add more compost around the base of the shoots.

You'll find potato tubers, including early, main, and storage varieties, in garden centers from the late winter on.

Early potatoes will take 14–15 weeks between planting and harvesting, main plantings 15–17 weeks, while storage potatoes will take 17–20 weeks.

Once harvested, you can store any sound storage tubers in paper or burlap bags. Brush the soil off, and leave them to dry in the sun for a few hours.

If you only grow one type, pick an early type for a quick supply of delicious baby new potatoes.

1 "Chit" the tubers
If you "chit" the tubers, it encourages new shoots. It's not essential, but it does speed up growth. Place the tubers in an egg carton so most of the "eyes" are at the top. Leave in a cool, light spot for a few weeks.

2 Plant in compost
Place a punctured black refuse bag inside the sack, and add 6in (15cm) of compost. Space out three sprouted tubers, being careful not to snap the fragile shoots, then cover with compost.

3 "Earth up"
As leafy shoots extend, "earth up" by adding more compost to just below the shoot tips, rolling up the sack gradually. This stops light from reaching the tubers, which turns them green and inedible.

TIMELY ADVICE

❋ **Start them off** Chit early varieties in late winter. For even earlier crops, plant and protect the tubers in a greenhouse.

❋ **Feed storage varieties** These may run short of nutrients, so feed every two weeks during summer with a general liquid fertilizer. Early types shouldn't need feeding.

❋ **Avoid splashback on leaves** Water beneath the foliage to lessen the risk of diseases such as blight.

❋ **"Earth up"** This will cover some of the plant's green leaves, but don't worry—new shoots will soon appear.

❋ **Harvest** Early potatoes can be harvested when they flower, but leave storage crops until the leaves start to yellow. Gently feel the tuber size in the soil before harvesting.

4 Prepare to harvest

Water regularly during the growing season. Once the plants are ready to harvest, cut open the bag with scissors to reach the potatoes.

Homemade compost

Good compost can make all the difference to the quality of your soil and the health of your plants. You can buy bags of it from garden centers, but why bother when you can make it yourself using your own organic material?

IDEAL COMPOST COMPOSITION

Perfect compost is produced when there is the right balance of brown (carbon-rich) and green (nitrogen-rich) materials within the heap. A 50:50 ratio is ideal for bacteria and micro-organisms to work their magic.

GREEN
This is the "soft" waste; including leaves, annual weeds, raw kitchen waste, and uncooked fruit and vegetable trimmings.

BROWN
This "hard" waste includes shredded woody plant stems and prunings along with paper, cardboard, and straw.

GRASS CLIPPINGS
Too much grass stops micro-organisms from working well, so mix grass with shredded brown and green waste before adding.

LEAF MOLD

If you have a lot of trees in or around your garden, gather the leaves up in the fall, and put them into sacks or bags. Leave in an out-of-the-way corner of your garden, and after one or two years you will have perfect, crumbly compost.

BAGS OF COMPOST
Put leaves in thick plastic bags, and moisten if dry. Pierce holes in the bag, and set aside to rot.

TURNING AND EMPTYING

❋ **Mix it up** Turning the materials in the compost heap helps incorporate air, which is vital for the composting process. If the materials in the heap become too wet or compacted, composting is much slower.

❋ **Emptying the heap** Compost can be ready in six months if left over the summer, when it rots more rapidly. The compost is ready to use when it is dark brown with a crumbly, soil-like texture. Use from the bottom of the bin first.

BRIGHT IDEAS

Compost can be made in a variety of receptacles, from closed bins to open heaps. Bins with a lid will produce more heat and therefore compost more quickly, but open heaps are much easier to turn. Choose your composting method according to how much space you can give to it, as well as how much waste material you are likely to want to compost.

STYLISH BEEHIVE

These pretty wooden bins are designed to look like traditional beehives. They are ideal for smaller gardens or where you need your bin to be aesthetically pleasing rather than an eyesore.

ROTATING TUMBLER

These plastic bins are available in many sizes to suit all gardens. The bins are attached to a frame that allows the gardener to rotate the bin, aerating and turning the material with minimum effort.

RECYCLED RECYCLER

Open, slatted bins can be made from wooden pallets. Line with bags that have been punched with air holes. Cover the compost with cardboard or carpet to help the heap heat up and cook nicely.

TOWER OF TIRES

This is a simple, economical way to make a compost bin. Many garages will happily give away used tires for free, which can be stacked to create a funky circular bin. As the heap grows, just add another tire!

COMPOST DOS & DON'TS

❋ **Do** place woody material at the base of the bin to help with air circulation.

❋ **Do** keep the bin moist in dry weather to help rot the materials.

❋ **Do** turn the bin, and cover it to increase the heat within the heap if you want to speed up the composting process.

❋ **Don't** add too much wet or soggy waste; it will upset the balance of the heap, and you will end up with a sludgy mess.

❋ **Don't** add large twigs and bits of cardboard to the heap—shred these materials first.

❋ **Don't** add cooked food to a compost heap—it will encourage vermin.

WORM COMPOST

If you only have a small garden or do not have much compostable waste, a worm compost is a good way to produce rich, homemade compost. Kitchen and garden waste is very quickly transformed into nutritious plant food. You just need some composting worms and a special bin, then let the worms do the rest!

CARING FOR YOUR WORMS

Avoid excess heat, cold, or wet. Don't overfeed, and draw off liquor (free concentrated fertilizer) regularly.

Better boundaries

Walls, fences, and hedges should provide a decorative backdrop to the garden as well as privacy, but boundaries and internal divisions are often in need of a mini makeover. Happily there are all kinds of quick and easy solutions that will pep up screens and partitions and make even dry or shady sites sparkle with flowering and foliage climbers and wall shrubs.

Hedge makeover

Hedges make attractive boundaries around or within gardens, and add color and texture. Whether high or low, hedges can provide a lush backdrop to other planting too, and if evergreen plants are used, provide interest and form in a winter garden. Whether informal or formal, hedging looks its best when it is healthy and in good condition. If your hedge is looking a little neglected, don't despair, a good trim will give it shape and style and encourage fresh new growth.

⊕ HEDGE TRIMMER

Powered hedge trimmers make light work of large hedges, but check for nesting birds first. Keeping the blade parallel to the hedge, use wide, sweeping movements, working from the bottom up. Always wear the correct safety gear, use sturdy ladders, and avoid overreaching.

⊕ SHEARS

Handheld shears are ideal for smaller hedges and those with small leaves. Getting a straight line on top of a formal, geometric hedge can be difficult, so attach a string to two vertical poles to act as a cutting guide. Keep the blades of the shears parallel to the top as you cut.

INSTANT IMPACT <<

❋ **Quick trim** If you don't have time to cut the whole hedge, take a pair of shears, and lightly and evenly snip along the top of the hedge to give it more definition.

❋ **Fill gaps** Fill small gaps where plants have died away in the hedge by taking a long branch from either side of the gap and tying them together to hide the hole. If the gap is large, then consider buying a mature specimen to replace the one that has died.

WAVY HEDGE
Wavy or cloud hedges look striking in an informal plan. Billowing shapes soften boundaries and lines within the garden. The perfect shape takes practice, but this relaxed style easily tolerates mistakes.

BATTERY-OPERATED HEDGE TRIMMER
Battery trimmers are a good option for gardens without an outdoor electric supply and are also relatively safe. Trimmers with cords cause many accidents because they are easy to get tangled up in. Small models save wrist strain when trimming topiary.

● TOPIARY SHEARS
To sculpt hedges into crisp shapes or figures, use sheep shears (left) or small-bladed shears. Both are perfect for precise trimming. Sheep shears are used one-handed, so rest frequently to reduce fatigue.

● HEDGE CLIPPINGS
Immediately remove hedge trimmings from the plant surface and base to prevent them from rotting and spreading disease. Run your hand or a long pole over the hedge to dislodge clippings.

>> IF YOU HAVE MORE TIME

❋ **Add shape** Create interest in a hedgerow by punctuating it with sculpted features. In informal hedges, create triangular finials or topiary animals.

❋ **Healthy hedging** Trim the sides of a tall hedge, making sure the sides slope slightly inward toward the top. The top of the hedge should end up narrower than the bottom. Cut this way, the hedge won't splay out when heavy snow settles, and the base receives more light.

Creative fences

Sprucing up fences is a big improvement. Start by replacing rotten posts, gravel boards, and broken panels. Add a touch of sophistication with toning paint-stains, and unify mismatched panels with the addition of screening or trellis.

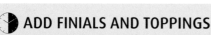 ADD FINIALS AND TOPPINGS

It's easy to upgrade existing fencing to add more character and charm to the garden. Simply mount fence caps and ball- or acorn-shaped finials to posts and paint, or attach trellis, retaining privacy but letting in light.

TOP NOTCH
Drill a hole through the fence cap and post, and screw in the acorn-shaped finial to finish.

FACE LIFT
Exterior paint-stain is best applied with a brush or small roller to untreated or weathered wood.

TRELLIS
Produce a lighter look by filling in the gap above solid panels with trellis. Secure with screws.

WILLOW FINISH
Use pre-soaked or fresh willow wands to weave a decorative edge for handmade trellis.

SCREENING

This versatile product comes in various finishes from dark rustic brushwood or heather to lighter willow, and finally traditional bamboo. Attach with a heavy-duty staple gun to cover mismatched fence panels or to create textured backdrops.

BRIGHT IDEAS

Make wooden screens, fences, and trellis panels work hard in the space they occupy by giving them a decorative or practical function. Get creative with paints, stains, sculptural elements, and plants. Below, red currant cordons with strawberries at their base provide both an ornamental and edible façade.

LAYERED LOOK

Transform a lackluster fence by attaching a roll of screening to create a plain backdrop and fixing a piece of decorative architectural trellis in front. Position a topiary standard in the foreground.

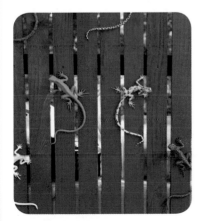

FUNKY FIXTURES

Provided they are waterproof and frost-proof, you can fix any colorful object to a fence using nails or transparent wire ties. Pick a theme and have fun!

PAINT PUNCH

Add punch to your patio by painting sections of screening or trellis in an eye-catching shade. Use as a stand-alone feature or as a backdrop for a flowering climber.

BROWN STUDY

Paint individual fencing planks in a variety of brown and gray shades to create a subtle contemporary backdrop for the garden— a great way to use up leftover wood stain.

Cool exposure

Cool, shady borders may not be drenched with sunlight from morning to evening, but that doesn't mean they can't be just as colorful as a sunny plot. Cooler exposures are the perfect home for shade-tolerant plants with variegated leaves and pale flowers, a variety of deciduous and evergreen shrubs, not to mention lush-looking woodland varieties.

GET THE LOOK

On one side of a water feature, plant one *Clematis henryi* (see how to on pp.150–151). On the other side, plant one ivy (*Hedera colchica* 'Sulphur Heart'). About 2–3ft (60–90cm) from the ivy, further away from the water feature, plant the rambler rose 'Albéric Barbier'. Plant your choice of Japanese maple (*Acer palmatum*) in the ivy's foreground so that the branches arch over, framing the fountain. On the other side, plant five to seven foxgloves.

CLEMATIS COLLECTION

Clematis such as *Clematis henryi* raise their heads to the sun but love their roots in the shade, so they are ideal for cooler sites. Plant in well-drained soil, and train up supports.

SHADY SHRUBS

Japanese maples, *Acer palmatum* cultivars, thrive in sheltered locations, where their leaves are protected from scorch. Red cultivars need some sun to develop their foliage color.

SELF-CLINGERS

Climbers such as ivy will happily romp up a wall without needing any training or support. Choose variegated ivies to lighten up a dark wall, such as *Hedera colchica* 'Sulphur Heart'.

COMPLETE THE LOOK

Natural light may be hard to find in a shady garden, but with a few clever tricks you can brighten up dark spots with plants and accessories.

✱ **Sparkling cascade** Water tumbling into a raised pool from a traditional pump will catch the light and glisten. If you prefer a modern look, stainless steel water sculptures have mirrored surfaces.

✱ **Poolside planting** Soften the pool edges, and brighten up hard landscaping with shade-tolerant, moisture-loving marginal or bog plants. Choose plants that won't outgrow their space too quickly and will shine in the shade, such as white flowers of *Zantedeschia* or golden-variegated foliage.

✱ **Fern focus** Ferns provide a lush backdrop to flowering plants, and evergreen ones will provide color and texture even in the winter.

✱ **Light touch** Focus on using tricks of the light. Use pale-colored flowers and foliage, and lay light paving slabs to reflect natural light.

MORE PLANT OPTIONS

CLEMATIS COLLECTION *Clematis alpina, C. macropetala, C. montana, C. 'Ernest Markham', C. 'Perle d'Azur', C. 'Jackmanii'*

SHADY SHRUBS *Jasminum nudiflorum, Hydrangea macrophylla, Choisya ternata 'Sundance', Skimmia japonica 'Rubella'*

SELF-CLINGERS *Parthenocissus henryana, Hydrangea anomala* subsp. *petiolaris, Hedera colchica* 'Dentata Variegata'

WOODLAND BLOOMS *Geranium nodosum, Geranium phaeum 'Album', Anemone* x *hybrida 'Honorine Jobert', Campanula persicifolia*

TOLERANT ROSES *Rosa 'Zéphirine Drouhin', R. 'Bleu Magenta', R. 'Danse du Feu', R. 'Madame Alfred Carrière', R. 'New Dawn'*

WOODLAND BLOOMS

Woodland plants such as foxgloves (*Digitalis* species) bring a splash of color to darker corners. They are at home in cooler exposures, preferring well-drained soil and shade.

TOLERANT ROSES

There is a good range of shade-tolerant roses available which will provide color and fragrance. White or pale-colored ramblers such as *Rosa* 'Albéric Barbier' lighten shady spots.

Warm exposure

This is the exposure that many gardeners dream of: a warm spot in which a multitude of popular or exotic plants will thrive with the minimum of fuss. A sunny, sheltered site is ideal for recreating a Mediterranean-style garden, which features an explosion of hot-colored flowers and foliage as well as climbers or feature plants dripping with citrus fruits and grapes.

🕐 GET THE LOOK

Against the wall, plant a grapevine (*Vitis vinifera*), choosing a suitably hardy one for your area (see pp.150–151 on how to plant a climber). To the right, place a potted Meyer's lemon. Further right, plant an outdoor peach variety like 'Peregrine' that is already trained onto a wooden fan. Attach the fan to wires. In front, plant five Maltese cross (*Lychnis chalcedonica*) and in front of them, slightly left, plant three *Dahlia* 'David Howard'.

BOUNTIFUL VINES
Grapevines can be successfully grown outdoors in all but the coldest areas. There are plenty of hardy varieties that will bear abundant fruit on a hot and sunny wall.

JUST PEACHY
Store-bought peaches will never be good enough once you've tasted homegrown fruit. A sunny wall and winter protection will reward you with a delicious harvest.

TROPICAL HARVEST
Nothing beats the fragrance of citrus flowers on a summer's day. Heat-loving limes, lemons, and oranges need lots of sun and must be taken inside in the winter to fruit another day.

COMPLETE THE LOOK

Bring a Mediterranean feel to your garden with just a few well-placed features, and on a sunny day you will find yourself transported miles away.

❋ **White walls** Crisp white walls are a trademark of homes in hot countries, and when the sun is reflected off of them, they create the perfect light backdrop for dark foliage.

❋ **Touch of terra-cotta** If you can't top your walls with warm terra-cotta tiles, include this texture and color in your plan by placing large clay pots along paths, on balconies, or as features set in beds and borders.

❋ **Smart shutters** You can replicate this Mediterranean look by fixing wooden shutters to a wall. These fake shutters can be sealed shut, or you can open them to reveal a mirror behind, which will reflect the planting in front.

❋ **Constant color** Keep the space warm and bright by including hardy plants that will provide foliage or flowers year-round.

MORE PLANT OPTIONS

BOUNTIFUL VINES Grape 'Brandt', 'Perlette', 'Phoenix', 'Pinot Noir', 'Siegerrebe', 'Boskoop Glory'

JUST PEACHY Peach 'Rochester', 'Peregrine'; Nectarine 'Lord Napier', 'Early Rivers'

TROPICAL HARVEST Meyer's lemon (*Citrus* x *meyeri* 'Meyer'), 'Garey's Eureka'; Tahiti lime (*Citrus* x *latifolia*); Orange 'Washington'; Calamondin 'Tiger'

HOT FAVORITES *Crocosmia* 'Hellfire', *Dahlia* 'Grenadier', *Canna indica*, *Achillea* 'Paprika'

VIVID FLOWERS *Hemerocallis* 'Corky', *Helenium* 'Moerheim Beauty', *Achillea* 'Walther Funcke', *Rudbeckia fulgida* var. *sullivantii* 'Goldsturm'

HOT FAVORITES

Once dismissed as dowdy, dahlias are enjoying a well-deserved return to popularity, and the orange blooms and dark foliage of *Dahlia* 'David Howard' are very much in style.

VIVID FLOWERS

The red Maltese cross (*Lychnis chalcedonica*) vies for attention with other plants in this design. Happiest in sunny, moisture-retentive soil, it blooms for weeks if deadheaded.

Planting climbers

Taking extra care when planting and training climbers allows them to grow and establish quickly and cover the fence, wall, or trellis more evenly. Most climbers race to the top of their support to reach the sunniest spot, so if you leave them tied to their original poles, they do just that. With all the plant's resources feeding the growth running along the top of the fence, the base loses foliage.

To have a strong, bushy plant, pruning at planting time helps, though it might seem rather drastic. It's particularly useful with wilt-prone, large-flowered clematis, too. Cut back to about 12in (30cm) above ground level, just above a pair of large buds.

1 Provide support
Screw in vine eyes to your fence posts. You might need to drill pilot holes first. Thread galvanized training wire through the vine eyes, pull it taut, and secure. Space the wires every 18in (45cm).

2 Prepare the ground
Improve a broad area, digging in manure or compost and applying fertilizer. Dig a planting hole at least 18in (45cm) from the fence to avoid a dry "rain shadow" area. Add a fan of poles.

3 Plant the climber
Set the plant in the hole, tilting it backward so the poles touch the wires. The surface of the root ball should be level with the surrounding soil. Backfill and firm with your hands.

4 Re-attach stems
Undo stems from their poles and fan them out, attaching each to a new support pole with twine, using a figure eight. Tie above a bamboo joint to prevent it from slipping.

5 Mulch with bark
After giving the plant and surrounding soil a thorough soaking, apply several inches (centimeters) depth of bark mulch around its base. Keep a gap free of mulch around the neck of the plant.

MORE PLANT OPTIONS

❈ **Foliage effect** Golden hop (*Humulus lupulus* 'Aureus'); gold-leaf jasmine (*Jasminum officinale* 'Fiona Sunrise'); purple-leaf grapevine (*Vitis vinifera* 'Purpurea'); variegated Persian ivy (*Hedera colchica* 'Dentata Variegata')

❈ **Flower power** *Clematis* 'Bill MacKenzie'; *Clematis* Jackmanii Group e.g. 'Niobe'; *Clematis viticella* cultivars e.g. 'Polish Spirit' and 'Madame Julia Correvon'; passion flower (*Passiflora caerulea*)

❈ **Quick cover** Chinese Virginia creeper (*Parthenocissus henryana*); *Clematis montana* 'Elizabeth'; *Clematis tangutica*; *Lonicera japonica* 'Halliana'; rambler roses

❈ **Fragrance** Jasmine (*Jasminum officinale*); star jasmine (*Trachelospermum jasminoides*); white Chinese wisteria (*Wisteria sinensis* 'Alba')

Brightening walls

In areas where planting opportunities are limited, especially near the house, adding color by painting or staining walls and fences can create a lively atmosphere. Think about the mood or style you want to evoke and how elements apart from walls (e.g. doors, furniture, and structures such as pergolas), can be united using a limited color palette.

⏱ GET THE LOOK

Choose one wall for the bold feature color (see pp.86–87 for preparation tips). In sunny areas and hot climates, clear oranges, reds, and yellows work well but in cooler, cloudier regions and in shade, the light is blue-toned, so blue-reds like raspberry or maroon as well as burnt orange shades and rich blues glow effectively. Use a contrasting shade to highlight smaller elements such as furniture, doors, and trellis panels.

VIBRANT HIGHLIGHTS
Rich cornflower blue paint is used here to make a feature of the door, chair, and bench, providing a lovely cool contrast to the vibrant orange wall.

DECORATIVE DETAIL
A narrow border, created by setting in mortar lines of small, gleaming-white and polished-black pebbles, echoes the pebble patio and enhances the Mediterranean theme.

CONTRASTING TEXTURE
Exposed stone or brickwork surrounded by whitewashed treatment adds to the rustic charm of this courtyard and emphasizes windows and doors.

FINISHING TOUCHES

Using a particular palette often suggests a theme. The colors used here create a Mediterranean feel, which is further enhanced by the choice of furniture and decorative elements.

- ❋ **Add-on ornaments** A few blue and white china plates are wall-mounted as ornaments, but you could also feature a mosaic tile (see pp.40–41).
- ❋ **Climber-covered pergola** Shocking pink *Bougainvillea* casts dappled shade over the dining area. In frost-prone regions, use a hardier climber such as a grapevine or the evergreen *Clematis armandii*.
- ❋ **Chair lift** Bring new life to an old, worn kitchen chair or occasional table using bold blue exterior gloss paint over universal primer.
- ❋ **Pots and planters** Finish off by adding terra-cotta pots in various shapes and sizes, some planted and others left empty.

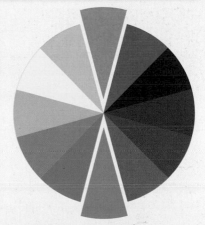

FEATURE COLOR
You don't need a lot of the bright wall color to really make a statement. This orange evokes sunshine and heat perfectly and is a ideal foil for the climbing *Bougainvillea*.

FABRICS AND FURNISHINGS
Here, the collection of cool, white chair covers mirrors the white walls, but plain or patterned fabrics can also work, bringing out other colors to link the design together.

COLOR WHEEL
Wheels are useful for showing which color combinations create the best effects. Here, cool blue has been used as a complementary highlight color to hot orange, on the opposite side of the wheel. Pick colors next to each other for a more harmonious effect.

Plant a boundary

There are locations where the views beyond the garden's boundaries are too beautiful to block out completely. While some sense of separation is desirable, with clever planting the garden can appear to extend far beyond its true extent. Soft plant dividers are also very useful for creating separate "rooms" within the garden.

🕐 GET THE LOOK

After thoroughly preparing the ground and pre-soaking all the plants, lay out the following: on the far right, one ornamental cherry and on the far left one purple smoke bush. In between, arrange a broad strip of five *Miscanthus sinensis* 'Malepartus' or similar on the left, and overlap with five *Molinia caerulea* subsp. *arundinacea* on the right. Behind the grasses dot five Joe Pye weed. Plant in prepared holes, water in, and add bark mulch.

HIGH RISE
The wildflower lookalike Joe Pye weed (*Eupatorium purpureum*) lifts its domed heads above the surrounding planting. Its blooms are a late treat for butterflies.

TREE LINE
The ornamental cherry (*Prunus*) provides a spectacular display of fall leaves and in the spring, produces dainty tresses of pink or white blossoms.

PROUD PLUMES
Turning darker as they age, the narrow plumes of eulalia grass (*Miscanthus sinensis* 'Malepartus') echo the darker purple foliage of the neighboring shrubs.

FINISHING TOUCHES

The planting in this border has been selected to enhance the woodland's fall display and to help draw the eye towards the "borrowed" landscape.

❋ **Filtered view** The flower stems and foliage of certain taller grasses and perennials allow you to see through to the area beyond yet still create a sense of enclosure.

❋ **Framed picture** Select sections of the view for framing using arching tree or shrub branches.

❋ **Woven layers** Arrange plants in long, overlapping bands to create an illusion of depth, allowing greater planting diversity within a relatively narrow border.

❋ **Hidden barrier** A low wire fence provides extra security along the property's boundary and is almost invisible once the foreground is planted.

RICH TINTS
In summer, cloudlike flower plumes appear on the purple smoke bush (Cotinus coggygria 'Royal Purple'). The rounded leaves develop rich tints before they drop in late fall.

GOSSAMER GRASSES
The see-through flower stems of plants like purple moor grass (Molinia caerulea subsp. arundinacea) and its varieties are perfect for creating soft boundaries.

MORE PLANT OPTIONS

HIGH RISE Rudbeckia laciniata 'Herbstsonne'; Echinops ritro; Verbena bonariensis; Veronicastrum virginicum 'Album'

TREE LINE Sumach (Rhus typhina); Prunus subhirtella 'Autumnalis Rosea'; Magnolia x soulangeana; Cotoneaster frigidus 'Cornubia'; Japanese crabapple (Malus floribunda)

PROUD PLUMES Aruncus dioicus; Calamagrostis x acutiflora 'Karl Foerster'; Cortaderia selloana 'Pumila'; Miscanthus sinensis 'Silberfeder'

RICH TINTS Physocarpus opulifolius 'Diabolo'; Cotinus 'Grace'; Photinia x fraseri 'Red Robin'; Cercis canadensis 'Forest Pansy'; Fothergilla major

GOSSAMER GRASSES Deschampsia cespitosa; Stipa gigantea; Panicum virgatum; Anemanthele lessoniana

Welcoming wildlife

Birds, bees, and butterflies add another dimension to the experience of gardening, and just by making a few subtle changes or additions to your planting design, you can dramatically increase your plot's wildlife quotient. You don't have to turn the borders over to weeds or sacrifice color and interest. Many plans and planting ideas, designed to attract a variety of creatures, also look terrific.

Wildlife habitat

Share your garden with some wildlife visitors, and you will be repaid in full. You can while away the days watching them and know that as they busy themselves in your garden, they are also reducing your workload!

⊕ WILDFLOWER AREAS
Encourage beneficial insects and pollinators including bees and butterflies into your garden by luring them to borders filled with their favorite plants.

⊕ TOADS AND FROGS
The ultimate gardener's friends, toads and frogs will happily munch on a wide range of insects and are particularly fond of slugs, so it's worth making space for them in your garden. Help them set up housekeeping by providing cool, dark places to hide in like clay pots, log piles, or stones around ponds.

⊕ WATER IN THE GARDEN
Water will attract a wide range of creatures and lots of insects. Insects draw dragonflies, birds, amphibians, and bats. Ensure your pond has a sloping side for safe access to the water. To make sure it is tempting for the creatures, position it in a sunny spot sheltered from strong winds.

INSTANT IMPACT <<

❋ **Don't be too tidy** Wildlife won't flock to a neat garden because it provides fewer opportunities for shelter. If you want visitors, keep pruning and clearing to a minimum.

❋ **Log pile** Dig a shallow trench in a shady corner, and pile up logs or pruned branches in it so that

some are slightly buried. Left undisturbed, beetles and other beneficial insects will soon make the logs their home.

❋ **Nectar source** Sow quick-growing, hardy annual flower mix in gaps in the border to provide nectar for bees and hoverflies.

◕ GREEN ROOF

Living green roofs not only make dull hard landscaping look attractive, but they also make ideal homes for beneficial insects. Grow plants on a prepared shed roof, or buy rolls of ready-made sedum matting.

◕ TREES AND HEDGES

Trees and hedges provide welcome spots for birds and other wildlife to nest, forage for food, and take shelter from weather and predators, so do a thorough check for nesting animals before pruning.

◕ ROOSTING POUCH

Made from natural materials, these hanging pouches provide a safe and cozy home for little birds away from harsh weather and predators. Hang or fix to a tree in a sheltered spot out of prevailing winds and full sun.

◕ SMALL ANIMAL HOUSE

Place a wooden box or house in a quiet corner, and it won't be long before a wild creature takes up residence.

>> IF YOU HAVE MORE TIME

❋ **Planning more habitats** Spend time in your garden thinking of and planning ideal sites for nest boxes, wildlife ponds, or bog gardens.

❋ **Plant a perch** If your garden is relatively new, plant quick-growing or mature shrubs or a small tree to provide safe vantage points for birds.

❋ **All access pass** Check boundaries lines, and ensure fencing has large enough gaps at ground level for small visiting animals to come in and out.

Mini bog garden

YOU WILL NEED

Bamboo cane and string

Plastic sheeting

Well-rotted manure or garden compost

Pebbles

Moisture-loving plants (e.g. Chinese rhubarb (*Rheum palmatum*), *Hosta*, fiber optic plant (*Isolepis cernua*), *Acorus gramineus* 'Variegatus', Japanese water lily (*Iris ensata*), *Lysimachia ciliata* 'Firecracker', *Houttuynia cordata* 'Chameleon')

A bog garden is the perfect alternative to a pond if you have young children. It also provides a great habitat for frogs, toads, and salamanders. They not only find shelter among the lush canopy of foliage but also relish the moisture and ready food supply.

Put a bog garden next to a pond, and you have the best of both worlds, including a retreat for emerging young frogs. The moist ground allows you to grow a wide range of wildlife-friendly flowers, providing nectar and pollen for bees and other insects.

Add plenty of well-rotted manure or homemade compost to your bog garden before you plant to improve the soil's capacity to hold moisture.

1 Choose your location

Pick a spot in good light. A natural hollow is ideal. If next to a pond, ensure that water run-off can't enter the pond since it will overfertilize the water and encourage algae. Mark out a circle.

2 Prepare the ground

Remove grass, weeds, and plants. Pile soil nearby to use for backfilling. Excavate a depression deep enough to plant the largest rootball at the center.

3 Lay out the liner

Spread a single sheet of plastic in the hole. The bog garden must have drainage, so puncture the center of the sheet several times with a fork. Backfill with a mixture of manure and excavated soil.

4 Plant moisture lovers

Avoiding walking on the soil, plant a big-leaf plant like Chinese rhubarb (*Rheum palmatum* 'Atrosanguineum'), and surround with moisture-loving plants. Edge with pebbles.

5 Water thoroughly

It will take a while for the soil to settle, but don't try to flatten out any unevenness or press down too hard on the soil because this will adversely affect the drainage. Water well.

SUITABLE PLANTS

- ❋ *Astilbe*
- ❋ **Bowles's golden sedge** (*Carex elata* 'Aurea')
- ❋ **Bugle** (*Ajuga reptans*)
- ❋ **Candelabra primulas** (*Primula pulverulenta, Primula beesiana, Primula bulleyana*)
- ❋ **Dwarf umbrella plant** (*Darmera peltata* 'Nana')
- ❋ **Joe-Pye weed** (*Eupatorium maculatum*)
- ❋ *Ligularia* 'The Rocket'
- ❋ *Ligularia dentata* 'Desdemona'
- ❋ **Purple loosestrife** (*Lythrum salicaria* 'Blush')
- ❋ **Ragged robin** (*Lychnis flos-cuculi*)
- ❋ *Stachys palustris*
- ❋ **Water avens** (*Geum rivale* 'Leonard's Variety')

Planting for bees

Bees buzz over wild gardens, so allow the base of a mixed hedge to fill with leaf litter and "weeds," and grow nectar- and pollen-rich flowers together with a variety of meadow plants and cornfield annuals.

◕ BEE HOUSES

Site bee houses in a sunny, sheltered spot close to a good nectar and pollen source. Some solitary bees lay eggs in bore holes in wood, and bumblebees often use abandoned rodent nests or cavities underground.

BEE PLAYGROUND
The habitat stack (above) offers shelter and nesting sites for bees and other small creatures. Arrange bricks, roof tiles, drainage pipes and drilled blocks of wood in layers using old untreated planks for support. Fill potential bee nests with hay, fleece and hair from animal grooming.

◕ MAKE IT

✻ **Bee hotel** Mason bees lay eggs in hollow stems, so gather up some bamboo poles, and make the perfect bee bolt hole. Put modeling clay in the base of a clay pot, cut short lengths of bamboo poles, and press as many as you can into the clay. In spring, suspend from trees or from hooks in your borders.

PERFECT PLANTS

To draw the bees in, grow single-flowered, English-garden perennials such as delphinium, poppy, verbascum, campanula, polemonium, and scabiosa; hardy annuals like *Phacelia*, and wildflowers. Most flowering herbs are irresistible too.

CRANESBILL
A classic English-garden perennial, common varieties like *Geranium* 'Johnson's Blue' are always buzzing with bees.

BLANKET FLOWER
The two-toned *Gaillardia* cultivars bloom for months in summer if regularly deadheaded and are bright bee and butterfly attractors.

PLUME THISTLE
Cirsium rivulare 'Atropurpureum' is a less prickly relative of the wild thistle, which flowers in the summer. It likes moisture-retentive soil.

EARLY BLOOMERS

These plants are vital for the survival of emerging queen bumblebees after hibernation.

Aubrieta deltoidea; *Ajuga reptans*; comfrey (*Symphytum officinale*); crocus; *Cytisus* x *praecox*; forget-me-not (*Myosotis*); foxglove (*Digitalis purpurea*); fruit trees; grape hyacinth (*Muscari*); hazel (*Corylus avellana*); *Helleborus*; pieris; *Primula vulgaris*; *Pulmonaria saccharata*; rhododendron; *Ribes sanguineum*; *Rosmarinus officinalis*; *Skimmia japonica*; *Viburnum* x *bodnantense*; *Salix*; winter heathers (*Erica*)

LAVENDER

These fragrant, aromatic herbs are the bee's favorite. Use a range of varieties in any sunny, well-drained spot to increase the spread of flowering. English lavenders are hardier and will self-seed into gravel and paving cracks.

FRENCH LAVENDER
Lavandula pedunculata subsp. *pedunculata* blooms all summer, and *Lavandula stoechas* plants have tufted blooms.

LAVENDER
Varieties of *Lavandula angustifolia* flower from mid- to late summer and come in a range of pastels.

Homegrown bird food

Herbaceous borders and prairie-style plantings offer many foraging opportunities for seed-eating birds in fall and winter. Simply stop deadheading in late summer to allow plants to form seedheads. Large swathes of one plant are an even bigger draw for visiting flocks.

PLANT IT

The seedheads of these plants are extremely attractive to birds. Combine 3–5 of each with ornamental grasses such as *Calamagrostis* x *acutifolia* 'Karl Foerster' and *Stipa gigantea* in a sunny corner of the garden, adjacent to cover from larger shrubs, or add groups of 3–5 in a herbaceous or mixed border.

RUDBECKIA

Single types of annual *Rudbeckia hirta* are available as young plants in early summer.

COSMOS

This tall annual is sold in divided trays in spring or as pot-grown plants later in the year.

CONEFLOWER

Echinacea purpurea, a perennial that flowers through summer, thrives on fertile, not-too-dry soil.

SOW IT

Some plants are hard to find in garden centers but easy to grow from seed. Sow most hardy annuals and hardy biennials, e.g. teasel (*Dipsacus fullonum*) and evening primrose (*Oenothera biennis*), direct into prepared soil (spring–early summer). Choose single flowers over doubles.

SUNFLOWERS

Sow medium-height and tall sunflowers individually in small pots or divided trays in spring.

MAKE IT

❋ **Seed treats** Melt suet, and mix with bird seed. Place around pine cones or in small pots threaded with string. Harden in the freezer before hanging outside.

❋ **Fruit and nuts** Use a darning needle to string up dried fruit and nuts. Slice fallen apples, and link them together with string.

❋ **Sunflowers** Cut off deadheads, thread with string, and hang up.

PERFECT PLANTS

Even a single berrying or fruiting plant is a valuable resource for birds. Many are also highly ornamental, making it easy to justify adding one or two to smaller urban plots. Shrubs, trees, and climbers not only offer food but also shelter and nesting sites. It's best to grow ornamental forms of natives, but most birds will adapt and rarely reject any glistening red or black fruits.

BERRIES
Plant a single cotoneaster shrub at the back of the border, or use *Cotoneaster horizontalis* against a wall or fence. For a thorny barrier, plant firethorn (*Pyracantha*) or barberry (*Berberis thunbergii*).

FRUITS
Single-flowered *Rosa rugosa* makes an excellent informal hedge or border specimen; finches love to break open the large hips in fall. Also try ornamental crabapples (*Malus*).

CLIMBERS
Cover walls, fences, and garden buildings with fragrant honeysuckle (*Lonicera periclymenum*), which later develops glistening red berries. Mature ivy (*Hedera helix*) has bird-friendly black fruit.

TREES
As well as planting a lawn or boundary specimen of a berrying tree like rowan (*Sorbus*), consider smaller ornamental conifers and other cone-bearing plants (e.g. birch, alder) as a source of seeds.

Winter bird care

As winter sets in, plants die down, and the ground hardens with a coating of frost or snow. It becomes difficult for birds to forage for the food and water they need to survive until spring. In these chilly conditions, birds must build up their fat deposits to keep warm, so high-energy foods should be on the menu. In the morning and the hours just before dusk, put food in a place where birds can safely access it, and ideally position feeders out of the reach of squirrels.

◗ BIRD TABLE

The simple bird table is one of the most effective ways to feed birds, especially the less agile ground feeders. Ensure the one you buy or build has drainage and a raised rim to prevent food from sliding off. A roof gives some protection from predators plus shelter from the rain. Clean regularly.

◗ SUET BALLS

You can buy suet balls ready-made or prepare them yourself with seeds and melted suet. Thread string through the bottom of a yogurt container, and pack in the ingredients. When set, cut away the pot and hang. Never use mesh-covered balls; these can trap the birds' feet or beaks and injure them.

INSTANT IMPACT <<

❋ **Nesting boxes** Buy a wooden birdbox, and attach it to a wall or fence, or fix to a tree in a safe, sheltered spot out of direct sunlight. They make cozy winter roosts too.

❋ **Edible wreath** Give the birds a Christmas wreath. Thread bits of apple, pear, orange, and some grapes onto a circular wreath frame, and hang in a tree.

❋ **Break the ice** Pour boiling water from the kettle onto frozen bird baths to melt the ice.

❋ **Ground feeders** Scatter apple pieces and broken suet cakes on a snow-cleared patch.

🐦 SEED FEEDER
Buy, fill, and hang a feeder. There is a huge range of bird seed, and seed-and-insect mixes available; some suited to general purpose or specialized bird feeders, others to tables or the ground.

🐦 BIRDFEEDER CARE
Clean and wash your birdfeeder regularly using hot soapy water with a drop of disinfectant added to remove harmful bacteria. Scrub and rinse well.

🐦 PEANUTS
Nuts are protein rich and high in fat, but when moldy contain a toxin that can kill birds. Only buy nuts from reputable suppliers, regularly empty and clean feeders, and never offer salted or roasted types.

🐦 BIRD BATH
Bathing is vital for maintaining cold-insulating feathers. Provide a dish with shallow sloping sides, such as a garbage can lid. Break ice, clean, and refill daily.

>> IF YOU HAVE MORE TIME

❋ **Eating station** Try to get ahold of a wooden post that has cracks or holes in it, but if you can't, drill some. Pack fatty foods such as suet into the holes so that birds can peck at them. Secure the post in the ground.

❋ **Rooftop living** If you want to encourage swallows, house martins, or sparrows to nest, get out the ladder and secure appropriate boxes (available from garden centers) just below the roof gutter.

Planting for butterflies

Many butterflies are becoming endangered, but you can do your part to encourage these beautiful creatures to enter your garden when deciding on your planting design. Choose their favorites, and create a butterfly paradise.

🕐 PLANT ON THE PATIO

If you want to get up close and personal, plant irresistible blooms in pots or in beds at the edges of patios. Butterflies will happily enjoy nectar from a variety of plants, so choose carefully to have flowers in bloom throughout the summer.

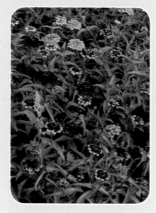

BUTTERFLY POTS

Verbenas and heliotrope are much loved by butterflies and are also long-flowering, providing them with food for many months. Plant trailing verbena in baskets and on the sides of large pots and raised beds. Blend heliotrope and jewel-colored, upright verbenas with compact, single-flowered cosmos varieties, bedding salvias, or tender lantana.

BEDDING FEAST

Gloriously colorful and vibrant zinnias are the sort of flowering plants that make both gardeners and butterflies happy. Their cheery flowers repeat through summer if deadheaded regularly. Other tempting bedding plants include fragrant wallflowers, single French marigolds, oregano, Mexican sunflower (*Tithonia*), single dahlias, sweet alyssum (*Lobularia maritima*), and lavender.

🕐 DRINKING

❊ **Nectar of the gods** The ultimate nutritious treat for butterflies is a saucer of washed sand saturated with water enriched with sugar syrup and manure. Leave it in full sun, and watch them flock in!

❊ **Standing room only** Ensure there is no surface water so butterflies can land on the sand.

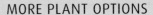

PERFECT PLANTS

Butterflies like to be warm, so grow plants that they find attractive in sunny beds. To keep these beautiful and beneficial insects visiting your garden, offer a good selection of plants to provide nectar from spring all the way through to fall. Spring flowers will pep up insects after winter hibernation, while fall ones will allow butterflies to build up essential food reserves.

LONG-STANDING FAVORITE

The tall stems of *Verbena bonariensis* provide nectar from spring until the first frost. These airy plants look elegant scattered through other plants or when used as a see-through screen.

ENGLISH-GARDEN STYLE

Centranthus ruber is an amazing sight when its flowers are covered in a haze of feeding butterflies. The rich red blooms appear from mid-summer until fall, when the plant will self-seed to get ready for another year.

MORE PLANT OPTIONS

SPRING FLOWERING *Aubrieta* 'Doctor Mules'; bluebells; grape hyacinth (*Muscari*); honesty (*Lunaria annua*); holly (*Ilex aquifolium*); Juneberry (*Amelanchier lamarckii*); lady's smock (*Cardamine pratensis*); wallflower (*Erysimum* cultivars)

SUMMER FLOWERING Heliotrope; *Phlox* species; bergamot; sea holly (*Eryngium* species); mullein (*Verbascum* species); hemp agrimony (*Eupatorium cannabinum*); purple loosestrife (*Lythrum salicaria*); ragged robin (*Lychnis flos-cuculi*); *Scabiosa caucasica* 'Clive Greaves'; sweet rocket (*Hesperis matronalis*); teasel (*Dipsacus fullonum*); *Verbena rigida*

FALL FLOWERING Ivy (*Hedera helix*); michaelmas daisy (*Aster novi-belgii*); *Sedum spectabile*; *Sedum* 'Herbstfreude'; black-eyed Susan (*Rudbeckia fulgida*); *Echinacea purpurea*; *Vitex agnus-castus*; *Caryopteris* x *clandonensis* 'Heavenly Blue'; *Scabiosa* 'Butterfly Blue'

BRIGHT AND SHOWY

The butterfly plant *Asclepias tuberosa* is a perennial, so it flowers reliably year after year. The 3ft- (90cm-) tall plant is topped by striking orange flowerheads and develops long seed pods in the fall.

DELECTABLE BEDS

Flowering from late summer into fall, hebes provide a late feast for butterflies. There are many different varieties, in shades and sizes to suit every garden, and their evergreen foliage is welcome in winter.

BUTTERFLY BUSH

Found along railways, roadsides, and on vacant land, buddlejas are tough plants that are easy to grow in any soil. Their dense panicles of multicolored flowers are paradise for butterflies into the fall.

Wildflower meadow

Even city dwellers can have a taste of the countryside in their urban gardens with a little planning and a few carefully selected native and garden plants. You don't need acres of space to create a wildflower meadow; you can mirror the effect in a border. A meadowlike design is a beautiful sight in the summer and once established will encourage birds, bees, and other beneficial insects.

● GET THE LOOK

Prepare the ground where you want to plant your wildflower meadow. The ideal spot will have good, well-drained soil in a sunny spot. Rake the soil to a fine tilth, and sow seeds in drifts to get an even distribution of plants—allow taller plants such as viper's bugloss and corn marigold to punctuate the design rather than grouping them at the back. Annuals provide first-year color while perennials and biennials establish.

WAVING TALL
The long stems of common yarrow (*Achillea millefolium*) hold clusters of delicate white flowers high above the other plants. In full sun, however, this perennial can be invasive.

SUN WORSHIPER
The corn marigold (*Chrysanthemum segetum*), once a familiar sight in wheat fields, is an annual that comes back year after year, provided the soil is turned over each fall.

FAMILIAR FRIENDS
The cheery white flowers of the perennial ox-eye daisy (*Leucanthemum vulgare*) are a common sight along roadsides and in meadows from late spring through summer.

FINISHING TOUCHES

Meadow meets urban garden. Here, the natural planting is offset by paving and stone seating, allowing visitors to enjoy the space without walking over plants.

❋ **Pathways** Create a walkway through the meadow so you can enjoy the planting. Formal paths are a chic, practical feature in a small, urban garden, or you can create a solid pathway with pieces of tree stumps, bark, or gravel.

❋ **Sit and savor** A wildflower garden in all its glory should be enjoyed. Place seating throughout the meadow so you can sit among the flowers. Stone seats add a contrast in texture, or use wooden benches or those made from willow or hazel for a more natural feel.

❋ **Add height** The trees in the wildflower beds add height to this design. The canopies and lower branches need to be trimmed to allow maximum sunlight to reach the plants. Rustic poles or pergolas can also add interest and height if you don't have room for trees.

MORE PLANT OPTIONS

WAVING TALL *Ammi majus*, cow parsley (*Anthriscus sylvestris*), giant scabiosa (*Cephalaria gigantea*), *Verbena bonariensis*

SUN WORSHIPER California poppy (*Eschscholzia californica*), *Cosmos bipinnatus*, teasel (*Dipsacus fullonum*)

FAMILIAR FRIENDS Corn cockle (*Agrostemma githago*), cowslip (*Primula veris*), field scabiosa (*Knautia arvensis*), poppy (*Papaver rhoeas*), red clover (*Trifolium pratense*)

SHADY CHARACTERS *Geranium macrorrhizum*, Japanese anemone (*Anemone x hybrida*), foxglove (*Digitalis purpurea*)

A HAZE OF BLUE *Campanula trachelium*, cornflower (*Centaurea cyanus*), meadow cranesbill (*Geranium pratense*)

SHADY CHARACTERS
This semi-evergreen, clump-forming perennial red campion (*Silene dioica*) is perfect for filling shady gaps. In addition, the pink flowers add welcome color from spring to fall.

A HAZE OF BLUE
The biennial viper's bugloss (*Echium vulgare*) is a tall bee magnet that adds a cool note to the design. Sow two years consecutively to have flowers each year.

Healthy pond

Not only are ponds a soothing spot for a gardener to while away a few hours on a warm day, but they are also a welcome home for a multitude of wildlife. However, no matter how informal your pond, it does demand care and attention to keep it looking its best and to provide a healthy habitat for any visiting creatures. Left untended, weeds and planting can take over, and decaying vegetation can taint the water and encourage unwanted algae and bacteria.

◑ STOP BLANKET WEED

A submerged bag of barley straw discourages troublesome algae. Use a bundle of about 1½ oz of straw per sq yd (50g per sq m) of water surface area for the best results. Lower the bundle in place in spring, and remove it in fall when it has turned black.

◑ CLEAR OVERGROWTH

Oxygenating plants are necessary in a healthy pond, but can be over vigorous and require thinning out routinely. Gently remove excess by gathering with a spring-tined rake. Pile onto the sides to allow creatures to slip back into the water overnight, and then compost.

INSTANT IMPACT <<

✳ **Elegant lilies** Waterlilies add a sophisticated touch to a sunny pond and a welcome splash of color. Choose a plant for the size of your pond.

✳ **Wind up weeds** To clear unsightly blanket weed, take a bamboo pole, insert it into the bulk of the algae, and turn it. The weed will wrap itself around the pole and can be simply lifted out. Leave it at the side of the pond overnight to allow insects to return to the water.

✳ **Night vision** If you enjoy wildlife-watching at night, position solar-powered spike lights around the edge of the pond.

CLEAN FILTER
In late fall, remove the pond filter, and clean with the hose to remove weeds or debris. Store away for the winter.

RAINWATER TOP-OFF
Wildlife ponds in particular benefit from being topped off with rainwater rather than tap water. Position water barrels near the pond where they can catch and store water, ready to be piped in when needed.

PLANTING UP
Lower deep-water plants into the pond in mesh baskets, which will allow them to take root. Covering the top of the compost with pebbles prevents the soil from dispersing into the water and clouding it.

REMOVE LEAVES
It is important to remove leaves from the water as they fall to keep them from decaying in the pond. Scoop them out with a net, or place netting over the pond surface at peak leaf fall, but remove it before winter.

>> IF YOU HAVE MORE TIME

❈ **Dividing marginals** The planting at the edges of the pond can get a little overcrowded over time. In spring, lift congested clumps of plants, and divide them into chunks. Replant the healthy roots, and compost the rest.

❈ **Slipway** If you want to encourage wildlife into your pond, make sure they have easy access to the water. Build pebble slopes for them to walk down, and position large stones at the edge for sunbathing creatures.

Easy care

There are plenty of time- and labor-saving ideas that help make gardening a more enjoyable and productive pastime. Knowing how to do the minimum amount of maintenance at the right time will produce maximum results. There are also techniques for cutting back on routine jobs like feeding and watering, as well as ways to streamline annual activities such as pruning—all of which will give you more time to relax and enjoy your garden.

Automatic irrigation

YOU WILL NEED

Irrigation "starter kit"
including an outside tap adaptor

Tape measure

Utility knife for cutting pipework,
plus cutting board

Hammer

Outdoor tap adaptor (only necessary to
purchase if one in kit doesn't fit tap)

Large cable clips with nails

If keeping patio pots and hanging baskets properly watered is becoming a chore, a small automatic watering system is invaluable. Add a watering computer or timer to your tap, and you can even program the water to come on while you are not home, or in the middle of the night—no annoying water drips. Watering in the cool of the evening is important because it reduces the amount of water lost through evaporation.

Automatic drip nozzle irrigation is very efficient since the water has time to slowly penetrate, rather than running off and over the edge of the container before it has soaked in.

1 Attach the pipe to the tap

Screw or snap in the fixture to your outdoor tap, and then spread out the tubing, laying it out to be certain that it will reach the various pots, planters, and baskets easily.

2 Connect the pipes

Loosely secure main tubing in position, but don't cut off the excess yet. Attach branches to it, using the T-joints. If they are difficult to insert, soften the pipe ends in a bowl of hot water.

3 Place one end in first pot

After measuring, cut side branches to the right length using a utility knife, allowing some extra leeway. Attach the drip nozzle to the end of the pipe, and push the plastic peg into the soil to secure.

4 Run pipe into next pot

Here, we've put the end of the main pipe into the topmost basket, fixing a drip nozzle, but you could put a stopper on for future extensions, and run a side branch to the basket instead.

5 Attach pipe to pergola

Tuck the pipework into spaces alongside paving and decking, and use cable clips to attach to any fence and trellis panels and up and along the framework of the pergola.

6 Insert into last basket

Put the final drip nozzle in place. A "thirsty" basket like this one containing tumbling tomatoes will enjoy regular watering. Adjust the duration and frequency of irrigation to avoid waste.

Lawn makeover

A glorious green expanse looks stunning in any garden design, but a lawn needs a fair bit of maintenance and care to keep it looking at its best. However, each of the tricks of the trade for creating a lush carpet are quick to perform and often have lasting results—and several only need to be done at certain times of the year rather than on a regular basis.

AERATING

Compacted soils have had all the air spaces trampled out, so grasses find it difficult to grow through. Spiking the lawn in the fall creates airways for healthy roots.

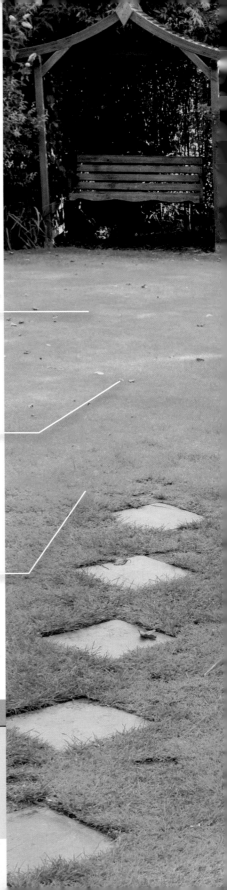

RAKING UP LEAVES

Clear away leaves as they fall onto your lawn, using a spring-tined rake. If left, a layer of leaves will smother the grass and weaken its growth. Collect the leaves as you go, and put them into perforated plastic sacks with a little water—in a year you will have nutritious leaf mold.

MOWING

It doesn't take long to run a mower over a lawn, with satisfying results. To keep grass healthy, don't cut it too short. Grass cut very short grows quickly and therefore requires more mowing. In hot weather, raise mower blades to high to prevent scorching the grass.

INSTANT IMPACT <<

❈ **Brush away worm casts** Worms are a sign of a healthy lawn, but the casts they leave on the surface do not look good. Brush away with a stiff broom on a dry day.

❈ **Rake out moss** A quick, vigorous work-over with a spring-tined rake will remove lurking moss. The lawn may look a little battered at first, but within days it will perk up.

❈ **Tidy steps** If you have stepping stones or a path set in the grass, a quick trim to redefine the edges will lift the overall appearance of a lawn. Remove turf strips and clippings.

⏱ TOP-DRESSING

A generous application of a top-dressing mix will help iron out lumps and bumps and improve the soil texture. Evenly scatter over some sandy compost mix with a spade, then brush it into the surface.

⏱ EDGING

Trim margins with edging shears for a sharp look and to clearly define where the grass ends and the borders begin.

⏱ SPOT WEEDING

Flat, rosette-forming weeds hide from the blades of the mower and need hands-on treatment to get rid of them. Use an old knife, or paint selective weedkiller onto individual plants to kill roots.

⏱ SEEDING PATCHES

In areas where the grass is sparse or worn away, sow new seed to fill the gap. Rough up the soil surface with a fork, and evenly scatter over the seeds. Cover with netting to protect from birds, and water in well.

>> IF YOU HAVE MORE TIME

❋ **Scarify** Thatch (old grass, dead moss, and other plant debris) can build up and smother the grass. In the fall, thoroughly rake it out with a spring-tined rake, or rent an electric scarifier.

❋ **Repair worn edges** Slice out damaged edges using a spade, and lift them away from the soil. Turn the piece around so the tattered edge is facing in, and firm it into place. Seed the patch, and trim the new edge.

"Beat the drought" border

If you have a sunny garden on free-draining soil, using drought-tolerant plants makes a lot of sense. With water supplies under increasing loads, the less water we use in the ornamental garden, the better.

Many alpines, shrubby and carpeting evergreen herbs, as well as Mediterranean shrubs and perennials have excellent drought-resistance. A sunny border set up as shown here not only cuts down on watering but also reduces weeding.

The permeable matting allows rainwater to penetrate but, especially with the addition of a light-reflecting surface mulch, also helps to keep the soil cool by trapping moisture around the plant roots.

Don't lay the gravel too thickly, or it will then trap moisture, which creates good conditions for weed seeds to germinate.

1 Turn over the ground
Dig the area to below the depth of the largest plant's rootball, breaking up any large clods and working in some grit or gravel for drainage if the soil has a high clay content.

2 Lay the weed matting
Level the soil to reduce the risk of water pooling, then cover with the matting, overlapping the pieces generously. Roughly trim to size, and fold the edges over.

3 Lay out the plants
Using long pieces of wire, peg down the folded edges. Bend over the tops of the wire to grip the matting. Keeping the plants in their pots, decide how you want them arranged in the border.

TIMELY ADVICE

❅ **Water in the first summer** The root systems of the plants might not yet be sufficiently developed to cope with drought, so water in the first summer during any hot, dry spells.

❅ **Lightly clip for shape** After lavender bushes and helianthemum have flowered, use shears to take off the old flowers and flower stems and a little of the soft shoot tips. This keeps plants bushy and compact.

❅ **Deadhead** Daisies need regular deadheading and removal of the flower stalks to encourage more blooms.

❅ **Weed** Remove weed seedlings in gravel before they form a large root system since they are much easier to pull out when tiny. It also doesn't give them time to flower and self-seed.

4 Cut planting holes

Mark the positions of the plant pots using a piece of chalk. Cut cross-shaped holes at each marked point with scissors, fold back the corners of the matting, then plant through the holes using a trowel.

5 Remove excess soil

Work soil around each rootball, removing excess to a bucket. Firm lightly. Replace the folded-back matting, and use a hand brush to sweep away soil crumbs.

6 Disguise with gravel

Water thoroughly. Cover the matting with just enough gravel to camouflage it, lifting the foliage to work the gravel underneath.

Late winter pruning

This is a useful time to make a start on pruning since the garden is relatively quiet workwise. In mild spells you can cut many mid- to late summer flowering, hardy, deciduous shrubs and climbers, including wisteria, as well as shrubs that are grown for their foliage or colored stems.

CLEANING TOOLS

Keeping tools in good order makes pruning easier and reduces the risk of spreading disease. Clean debris, sap, or rust off of blades, sterilize with rubbing alcohol, and oil with a lubricating, anti-corrosion product.

SHEARS
Scrape off any solidified sap with a razor blade, then rub with steel wool.

PRUNING SAW
Remove sawdust from the blade with a stiff brush, then oil with a rag.

PRUNING DOGWOOD

Act now if you have plain-leaf dogwoods grown for their colorful bark, including the scarlet-stemmed *Cornus alba* 'Sibirica', multi-toned *Cornus sanguinea* 'Midwinter Fire' (pictured), and mustard yellow *Cornus sericea* 'Flaviramea'. Cut before the leaf buds start to swell. New, non-flowering wood is the brightest; cutting back hard will encourage fresh growth to shoot up from the base.

SHORTEN
Begin with a general cutting back, shortening and thinning out last year's growth so that you can see where to cut next. Remove dead or damaged wood and crossing branches.

BASIC FRAMEWORK
Reduce the bush to a low framework of branches as shown, cutting to just above a pair of buds. New growth shoots from these.

BUSH AND PATIO ROSES

Cut growth back by a quarter to half, creating an open framework as shown. Remove dead or diseased parts, and spindly and crossing branches. Pick off old leaves.

PRECISION CUTS
Angle the cut to allow rainwater to run off. Cut to just above an outward-facing bud where possible.

WEATHER GUIDELINES

The main rule of thumb is to watch the weather forecast and avoid pruning and cutting back during frosty or snowy periods. Your local weather and climate may differ from elsewhere, so watch for signs of regrowth such as buds swelling, and take action.

DECIDUOUS FOLIAGE SHRUBS

For larger, more intensely colored leaves, prune back relatively hard, concentrating on removing a proportion of older stems.

Acer negundo 'Flamingo'; ornamental elder (*Sambucus*); *Physocarpus opulifolius* e.g. 'Dart's Gold', 'Diabolo'; *Berberis thunbergii* (colored leaf); *Salix integra* 'Hakuro-nishiki'; smoke bush (*Cotinus*); *Spiraea japonica*; *Weigela* (variegated cultivars); variegated dogwood (*Cornus*)

RAMBLER ROSES

Cut back now if you didn't prune in the fall, or if you have more radical pruning to do to rescue a rambler that has become overgrown.

Rosa 'Albéric Barbier'; *R.* 'Albertine'; *R.* 'American Pillar'; *R.* 'Bleu Magenta'; *R.* 'Blush Rambler'; *R.* 'Bobbie James'; *R.* 'Crimson Shower'; *R.* 'Félicité et Perpétue'; *R.* 'Kew Rambler'; *R.* 'Paul's Himalayan Musk'; *R.* 'Rambling Rector'; *R. filipes* 'Kiftsgate'; *R.* 'Seagull'; *R.* 'Veilchenblau'

HARDY LATE BLOOMERS

For larger blooms on the hydrangeas listed below, cut to a low framework of branches, otherwise just remove a third of oldest stems.

Hydrangea arborescens 'Annabelle'; *Hydrangea paniculata* e.g. 'Pink Diamond', 'Unique'; *Hypericum* 'Hidcote'; *Hypericum* x *inodorum* 'Elstead'; *Potentilla fruticosa* e.g. 'Abbotswood', 'Limelight', 'Primrose Beauty'; *Spiraea japonica* (flowering varieties); Clethra alnifolia

HARDY EVERGREENS

Cut to control size if necessary, after flowering and fruiting, and also if you want to train wall shrubs. Finish before nesting season starts.

Cherry laurel (*Prunus lauroceracus*); *Cotoneaster* x *watereri* and other cultivars; *Elaeagnus* x *ebbingei*; *Euonymus fortunei* 'Emerald Gaeity'; Firethorn (*Pyracantha*); *Garrya elliptica*; *Mahonia* x *media*; shrubby honeysuckle (*Lonicera nitida*); *Viburnum tinus* e.g. 'Eve Price'; yew (*Taxus baccata*)

BUSH AND PATIO ROSES

Hard pruning (see left) and removal of dead or black-spot infected stems and foliage keeps plants vigorous and healthy.

Rosa 'Amber Queen'; *R.* 'Arthur Bell'; *R.* 'Blessings'; *R.* 'Champagne Moments'; *R.* 'Fascination'; *R.* 'Ice Cream'; *R.* 'Indian Summer'; *R.* 'Many Happy Returns'; *R.* 'Margaret Merrill'; *R.* 'Royal William'; *R.* 'Ruby Anniversary'; *R.* 'Scarlet Patio'; *R.* 'Sweet Dreams'; *R.* 'Warm Wishes'

LATE-FLOWERING CLEMATIS

Cut these clematis back about 12in (30cm) from the ground, just above a strong pair of buds, or retain a larger branched framework.

Clematis 'Abundance'; *C.* 'Alba Luxurians'; *C.* 'Étoile Violette'; *C.* 'Gravetye Beauty'; *C.* 'Hagley Hybrid'; *C.* 'Huldine'; *C.* 'Jackmanii', *C.* 'Kermesina'; *C.* 'Little Nell'; *C.* 'Madame Julia Correvon'; *C.* 'Minuet'; *C.* 'Pagoda'; *C.* 'Perle d'Azur'; *C.* 'Polish Spirit'; *C.* 'Ville de Lyon'

Spring pruning

Pruning is really important now, but be guided by the weather in your area, and delay if spring is late and it is still cold and frosty outside. Early spring is ideal for finishing off bush roses and pruning climbing and repeat-flowering shrub roses. Later in spring, deal with spring-flowering plants and frost-vulnerable, late-flowering shrubs, shrubby herbs, and perennials.

PRUNING FAST AND LATE BLOOMERS

Many deciduous shrubs and climbers that flower in the midsummer bloom on wood produced the same year. You can prune these plants relatively hard in spring. Pruning keeps fast-growing, short-lived types youthful.

BUDDLEJA
Cut back the majority of last year's growth to a framework of healthy, well-spaced branches.

BUTTERFLY LURE
Reducing the bulk of a butterfly bush (*Buddleja davidii*) causes lots of new stems to sprout. These bear the honey-scented blooms.

HYDRANGEA PRUNING

Prune mop-head and lacecap hyrdangeas (*Hydrangea macrophylla* cultivars and hybrids) lightly, otherwise you remove the new year's flowering wood. Leave the heads on over winter to help protect buds from frost.

LARGE DOUBLE BUDS
Find a pair of large green swollen buds a little way back from stem tip. Cut just above. These buds become stems that bear flowers.

SHAPE UP
Cut away dead or frost-damaged wood, spindly stems, or crossing branches.

EARLY-SPRING ROSE PRUNE

Repeat-flowering bush roses flower on new wood; climbing and English roses grow on new shoots growing from a framework of older wood. Selective pruning in late winter and early spring triggers fresh growth and keeps plants healthy and vigorous. Improve results by mulching in late winter and feeding with granular rose food in spring.

SPUR PRUNING

Stimulate flowering shoots by cutting back old flowering stems that are growing off the main framework to two or three buds.

REPEAT-FLOWERING CLIMBERS

Tie in main branches to fill space, and cut back overlong shoots. Shorten last year's sideshoots to create spurs.

Rosa 'Aloha'; *R.* 'Compassion'; *R.* 'Danse du Feu'; *R.* 'Dublin Bay'; *R.* 'Étoile de Hollande'; *R.* 'Handel'; *R.* 'Parkdirektor Riggers'; *R.* 'Pink Perpétue'; *R.* 'Schoolgirl'; *R.* 'Swan Lake'; *R.* 'The New Dawn'

ENGLISH ROSES

Prune these repeat-flowering shrubs back by a quarter, shortening some sideshoots to a few buds and removing dead or diseased parts.

Rosa 'Abraham Darby'; *R.* 'Evelyn'; *R.* 'Gertrude Jekyll'; *R.* 'Golden Celebration'; *R.* 'Graham Thomas'; *R.* 'Jude the Obscure'; *R.* 'Mary Rose'; *R.* 'Molineux'; *R.* 'Scepter'd Isle'; *R.* 'Winchester Cathedral'; *R.* 'William Shakespeare 2000'

SHRUBS AND CLIMBERS

If you aren't sure how to prune a summer-flowering shrub, a good rule is to cut out about a third of the oldest wood in the spring. This is often a different color and texture from the newer stems. Don't prune spring- and early-summer-flowering shrubs until after they have flowered. Always check for bird nests before you start cutting.

HONEYSUCKLE

Contain by cutting back any long, straggly growth, and remove dead or damaged stems.

WINTER OR SPRING FLOWERING

Prune deciduous shrubs after flowering, removing a third of old wood or cutting flowered stems back (to base with *Kerria*).

Flowering currant (*Ribes sanguineum*); *Exochorda* x *macrantha* 'The Bride'; *Forsythia* x *intermedia*; *Kerria japonica*; *Prunus triloba*; *Spiraea* x *arguta*; winter-flowering honeysuckle (*Lonicera* x *purpusii* 'Winter Beauty'); witch hazel (*Hamamelis*)

GROWS FAST; FLOWERS LATER

Cut back summer-flowering shrubs, woody-based perennials, and shrubby herbs above regrowth at the base.

Abutilon x *suntense*; *Artemisia* 'Powis Castle'; *Caryopteris* x *clandonensis*; *Ceanothus* x *delileanus* 'Gloire de Versailles'; *Santolina chamaecyparissus*; curry plant (*Helichrysum italicum*); *Fuchsia* (hardy cultivars); *Penstemon*; *Perovskia atriplicifolia*; *Lavatera* x *clementii*

Summer pruning

Summer is ideal for pruning frost-sensitive evergreens so new growth has a chance to toughen before cold weather arrives. Prune early shrubs and climbers to encourage next year's flowering shoots. Prune long whippy shoots on wisteria to 5–6 buds from old stems. Remember to check for bird nests.

SHEARING LAVENDER

English lavender, (*Lavandula angustifolia*) needs clipping once it has flowered to keep plants bushy. Cut to 1in (1–2cm) above the woody part of the stem.

SPRING FALLBACK

If you don't have time to prune lavender in summer after it flowers, clip them in spring. Avoid clipping in winter since cold weather can damage any freshly cut shoots.

REPEAT FLUSHES

Use shears to cut back catmint (*Nepeta* x *faassenii*) and *Lamium maculatum* after each wave of flowering to encourage them to flower repeatedly.

FALL PRUNING RAMBLER ROSES

Rambler roses produce a great show in early summer and are very vigorous. In summer, tie in the supple new growth. In the fall, trim extra-long stems that have grown beyond the supports, and spur prune (shorten the shoots that have flowered to two or three buds.)

ROSE DEADHEADING

Cut off faded blooms, particularly from bush and repeat-flowering climbing roses, to keep plants flowering steadily.

EARLY BLOOMERS

Late spring- and early-summer flowering shrubs bloom on last season's wood so if you do need to prune, do it right after flowering so replacement shoots have time to mature.

CAMELLIA

These winter- and early spring-flowering shrubs need little attention. Summer prune to keep them within their space.

SHRUBS AND CLIMBERS

For those that flower in early summer, cut back flowered wood to strong new sideshoots, and cut out one-fifth of oldest wood to the base. Fresh growth will flower next summer. Lightly prune early climbers.

Beauty bush (*Kolkwitzia amabilis* 'Pink Cloud'); *Clematis alpina*; *Clematis armandii*; *Clematis macropetalla*; climbing hydrangea (*Hydrangea anomala* subsp. *petiolaris*); *Deutzia*; mockorange (*Phildelphus* 'Virginal'; shown); *Neillia*; *Weigela*

EVERGREENS

Shrubs with evergreen foliage are often vulnerable to frost damage on new growth, so pruning is usually avoided until after risk of frost has passed because cutting encourages a flush of new leaves.

SCREENS AND HEDGES
Trim hedges, screens, and shaped bushes. Clip evergreen azaleas lightly immediately after flowering.

EVERGREEN WITH WINTER DAMAGE
Warm spells and fall pruning promote growth flushes that may be damaged by late frost. Wait until danger of frost has passed before cleaning up damaged shoots or hard pruning.

Abelia; Aucuba japonica; boxwood (*Buxus sempervirens*); Californian lilac (*Ceanothus*); *Escallonia laevis* 'Gold Brian'; golden Mexican orange (*Choisya ternata* 'Sundance'); *Griselinia littoralis; Phormium; Photinia; Pieris japonica; Pittosporum*

FORMATIVE PRUNING AND TOPIARY
Even if topiary specimens like bay and boxwood have been scorched by harsh winter weather, delay clipping or shaping until there is no risk of frost. Finish clipping by the end of summer.

Boxwood (*Buxus sempervirens*); bay (*Laurus nobilis*); *Euonymus japonicus;* Japanese holly (*Ilex crenata*); myrtle (*Myrtus communis*); olive (*Olea europaea*); shrubby honeysuckle (*Lonicera nitida*); *Ligustrum delavayanum; Cupressus macrocarpa* 'Goldcrest'

FRUITING AND ORNAMENTAL TREES

Although traditionally pruned when fully dormant, many trees are best pruned in summer once all the leaves have opened and risk of sap bleeding from cuts has passed. This is because cuts heal more easily in summer, reducing the risk of die-back or infection. Summer is also ideal for pruning trained apples and pears because you can see where the fruits are forming and which parts are unproductive.

CHERRIES AND PLUMS
Both ornamental and productive forms of cherry and plum are susceptible to silver leaf disease, especially when pruned outside the summer growing period. Prune in midsummer.

TRAINED FRUIT
With espaliers, fans, cordons, and stepovers, as well as dwarf trees in pots, cut back unproductive leafy shoots (often growing vertically) in midsummer after the fruit has set.

ORNAMENTAL TREES
Remove or shorten unwanted branches. Take out any reverted (all-green) shoots on colored-leaf and variegated plants. Also cut out dead, crossing, and misplaced branches.

Index

Acknowledgments

THE AUTHOR would like to thank everyone on the *Gardening Shortcuts* editorial, design, and photography team at Dorling Kindersley, whose dedication and enthusiasm for the project was a terrific encouragement.

DORLING KINDERSLEY would like to thank the following for their help: Helena Caldon, Zia Allaway, Chauney Dunford, and Hilary Mandleberg for additional editorial help; Alison Shackleton and Becky Tennant for additional design help; Fiona Wild for proofreading; Michèle Clarke for indexing; Kate Johnsen for US editing; and Lori Spencer (US consultant).

PICTURE CREDITS The publisher would like to thank the following for their kind permission to reproduce their photographs:

(Key: a-above; b-below/bottom; c-center; f-far; l-left; r-right; t-top)

10-11 GAP Photos: Elke Borkowski (cl). **12-13 The Garden Collection:** Nicola Stocken Tomkins (c). **13 GAP Photos:** Mel Watson (cra). **14 GAP Photos:** BBC Magazines Ltd (clb, cb, crb). **15 GAP Photos:** BBC Magazines Ltd (clb, cr). **16-17 The Garden Collection:** Liz Eddison (clb). **18-19 The Garden Collection:** Marie O'Hara (ca). **22 Dorling Kindersley:** Lucy Claxton (ca). **22-23 GAP Photos:** John Glover. **24 Garden World Images:** Gilles Delacroix (cra). **24-25 The Garden Collection:** Nicola Stocken Tomkins (cr). **26 Garden World Images:** Richard Shiell (fcrb). **The Garden Collection:** Nicola Stocken Tomkins (clb, br). **27 Garden World Images:** Isabelle Anderson (br). **36 GAP Photos:** Hanneke Reijbroek (cb). **The Garden**

Collection: Nicola Stocken Tomkins (cl). **37 Sunny Aspects Ltd.** (clb). **38-39 The Garden Collection:** Nicola Stocken Tomkins (c). **44-45 Garden World Images:** Jenny Lilly (c). **46 Garden World Images:** Adrian James (tr). **46-47 The Garden Collection:** Nicola Stocken Tomkins. **48-49 The Garden Collection:** Derek Harris. **50 GAP Photos:** Gerald Majumdar (cra). **52 The Garden Collection:** Torie Chugg / Design: Clive Scott - RHS Hampton Court 07 (bl). **52-53 Garden World Images:** MAP / Nicole et Patrick Mioulane. **56-57 GAP Photos:** Richard Bloom. **58 Garden World Images:** Martin Hughes-Jones (bl). **58-59 GAP Photos:** Matt Anker. **60 Garden World Images:** MAP / Nicole et Patrick Mioulane (bl). **61 Garden World Images:** Ellen McKnight (bl). **64-65 The Garden Collection:** Nicola Stocken Tomkins. **70-71 The Garden Collection:** Nicola Stocken Tomkins. **74 John Woods Nurseries:** Hydrangea Endless Summer® The Bride (br). **78-79 GAP Photos:** Jerry Harpur. **79 Getty Images:** Friedrich Strauss / Garden Picture Library / Photolibrary (ca). **86 The Garden Collection:** Andrew Lawson / Mill Dene, Glos. (cb). **86-87 Marianne Majerus Garden Images:** Ali Ward. **87 Getty Images:** Juliette Wade / Garden Picture Library / Photolibrary (fcrb). **Marianne Majerus Garden Images:** Ali Ward (fclb). **90-91 IPC+ Syndication:** Mark Scott / Ideal Home. **95 Dorling Kindersley:** Angus Beare (cb). **The Garden Collection:** Liz Eddison / Designer: Marney Hall - Hampton Court 2001 (cra). **Marianne Majerus Garden Images:** Charlotte Rowe (cla). **99 Garden World Images:** Gary Smith (tr). **100 The Garden**

Collection: Liz Eddison / Design: Vivienne Walburn - Tatton Park 2007 (bc). **100-101 Dorling Kindersley:** Hampton Court Flower Show 2005, Designed by Guildford College, 'Journey of the Senses'. **101 Marianne Majerus Garden Images:** Gardens of Gothenburg, Sweden 2008 (tr). **102 Getty Images:** Georgianna Lane / Garden Photo World / Photolibrary (clb). **102-103 The Garden Collection:** Jonathan Buckley / Designer: Christopher Lloyd. **110 Dorling Kindersley:** Alan Buckingham (c). **111 Dorling Kindersley:** Alan Buckingham (crb). **114 Dorling Kindersley:** Alan Buckingham (c). **114-115 Garden World Images:** John Swithinbank. **118 The Garden Collection:** Andrew Lawson / Designer: Rupert Golby. RHS Chelsea Show. Country Living Garden (cb). **122 GAP Photos:** Martin Hughes-Jones (cb). **122-123 Marianne Majerus Garden Images:** The Old Vicarage, East Ruston, Norfolk. **135 Getty Images:** Photolibrary / Garden Picture Library / Linda Burgess (crb). **140-141 The Garden Collection:** Jonathan Buckley / Design: Bunny Guinness. **142-143 The Garden Collection:** Andrew Lawson / Old Rectory, Sudborough, Northants. **143 Corbis:** Harpur Garden Library (tc). **Dorling Kindersley:** Musee National de la Ceramique, Morocco (c). **144 The Garden Collection:** Jonathan Buckley / Design: Bunny Guinness (cra, fcr). **145 The Garden Collection:** Liz Eddison / Designer: Andrew Yates - Tatton Park 2003 (tl); Nicola Stocken Tomkins (cr). **148 Dorling Kindersley:** Alan Buckingham (bl). **The Garden Collection:** Torie Chugg (br). **152-153 Alamy Images:** Roger Cracknell 01 / classic. **152 Alamy**

Images: Roger Cracknell 01 / classic (bl, bc, br). **153 Alamy Images:** Roger Cracknell 01 / classic (bl, bc). **154 The Garden Collection:** Andrew Lawson (cb). **154-155 GAP Photos:** Clive Nichols. **158-159 The Garden Collection:** Jane Sebire / Design: Nigel Dunnett. **160 GAP Photos:** Elke Borkowski. **163 Alamy Images:** Igor Zhorov (cla). **164 Dorling Kindersley:** Unwins (fcl). **166-167 The Garden Collection:** Liz Eddison. **167 Dorling Kindersley:** Sean Hunter Photography (tc, c). **FLPA:** Gary K. Smith (ca). **168 FLPA:** Peter Entwistle (cr). **172 GAP Photos:** Michael King (c). **172-173 The Garden Collection:** Nicola Stocken Tomkins. **178-179 GAP Photos:** Carole Drake / Design Dave and Tina Primmer. **183 The Garden Collection:** Steven Wooster (tc). **184 Garden World Images:** N+R Colborn (cl)

Jacket images:
Front: **Marianne Majerus Garden Images:** Stephen Crisp t; *Spine:* **GAP Photos:** BBC Magazines Ltd

All other images © Dorling Kindersley

For further information see: **www.dkimages.com**